wonderful

WITHDRAWN

Weddings

for

cost-conscious

couples

Meredith₀ Books

Des Moines, Iowa

For Better or For Worse Wonderful Weddings for Cost-Conscious Couples

Editor: Amy Tincher-Durik
Writers: Jody Garlock, Kellie Kramer
Designer: Geoffrey Stevens
Copy Chief: Terri Fredrickson
Publishing Operations Manager: Karen Schirm
Edit and Design Production Coordinator:
Mary Lee Gavin
Editorial Assistants: Kaye Chabot, Kairee Mullen
Marketing Product Managers: Aparna Pande, Isaac Petersen,
Gina Rickert, Stephen Rogers, Brent Wiersma, Tyler Woods
Book Production Managers: Pam Kvitne, Marjorie J.
Schenkelberg, Rick von Holdt, Mark Weaver
Contributing Copy Editor: Amanda Knief
Contributing Proofreaders: Callie Dunbar, Sarah Enticknap,
Sue Fetters
Indexer: Elizabeth Parson
Illustrator: Daniel Pelavin

Meredith® Books

Executive Director, Editorial: Gregory H. Kayko
Executive Director, Design: Matt Strelecki
Executive Editor: Denise L. Caringer

Publisher and Editor in Chief: James D. Blume
Editorial Director: Linda Raglan Cunningham
Executive Director, Marketing: Jeffrey B. Myers
Executive Director, New Business Development:
Todd M. Davis
Executive Director, Sales: Ken Zagor
Director, Operations: George A. Susral
Director, Production: Douglas M. Johnston
Business Director: Jim Leonard

Vice President and General Manager: Douglas J. Guendel

Meredith Publishing Group

President: Jack Griffin
Senior Vice President: Bob Mate

Meredith Corporation

Chairman and Chief Executive Officer:
William T. Kerr
President and Chief Operating Officer:
Stephen M. Lacy

In Memoriam: E.T. Meredith III (1933-2003)

All of us at Meredith Books are dedicated to providing you with information and ideas to enhance your home. We welcome your comments and suggestions. Write to us at: Meredith Books, Home Decorating and Design Editorial Department, 1716 Locust St., Des Moines, IA 50309-3023.

If you would like to purchase any of our home decorating and design, cooking, crafts, gardening, or home improvement books, check wherever quality books are sold. Or visit us at: meredithbooks.com

For Better or For Worse Book Development Team

Roger Marmet, Executive Vice President & General Manager, TLC
Gena McCarthy, Executive Producer, TLC
Bruce Nash, Robyn Nash, and Debra Weeks, Executive Producers, Nash Entertainment
Sharon M. Bennett, Senior Vice President, Global Licensing
Carol LeBlanc, Vice President, Marketing & Retail Development
Jeannine Gaubert, Design Manager
Erica Jacobs Green, Director of Publishing
Cheryl King, Publishing Associate

Foreword

It takes a special bride- and groom-to-be to hand over the reigns of their wedding to family and friends and let them choose every detail—including the bride's dress—in just a week and with just $5,000. No way, you say? Impossible? A disaster in the making?

As host of the popular TLC series **For Better or For Worse**, I'm here to tell you that this seemingly unthinkable scenario is possible—and it can yield amazing results. In a time of skyrocketing wedding costs, this series has transformed the way engaged couples think about their weddings.

Which brings me to this book. I know many of you probably aren't going to relinquish complete control of your wedding to a team of family and friends, and you probably aren't attempting to execute your dream wedding in a week. But the creative and budget-friendly strategies revealed on **For Better or For Worse** can be applied to any situation. We've tapped ideas and advice from your favorite wedding planners on the series, and compiled this book to show you how you can have a wonderful wedding without sacrificing a thing or breaking the bank. But this is a book to USE as much as it is to read. You'll find sections to jot down your budget, guest list, and more. The project section is full of easy-to-make invitations, bouquets, and decorations, all designed by our talented wedding planners. And, true to the show, the pages are packed with fun and unique ways to personalize your special day, including ideas for finding off-the-beaten-path ceremony sites and pulling off theme weddings. All, of course, is done with budget-savvy couples like you in mind.

As you plan your big day, keep the following in mind: Everyone—your parents, your siblings, your friends—will voice opinions and expectations, but remember that this is about you. Remain true to who you are and what you want in your wedding, and ultimately your lives together. Whether your idea of bliss is a horse-drawn carriage taking you to the church or cocktails for 10 friends after courthouse vows, do whatever makes you feel special on your wedding day.

Congratulations on your engagement. Enjoy the ride that's about to ensue!

Alecia Davis

Alecia Davis
Host, **For Better or For Worse**

Contents

Meet the Experts   6
An introduction to the host and wedding planners of For Better or For Worse.

chapter
1 Getting Started   16
From budgeting to prioritizing, here's how to set your wedding plans in motion.

chapter
2 Creative License   60
Put your personal stamp on the big day with themes and beyond.

chapter
3 Shopping Smarts   74
From negotiating deals to securing contracts, here's what you need to know before you hit the stores.

chapter
4 Attire   124
Dressing for wedding-day success doesn't need to cost a fortune!

chapter
5 The Ceremony   146
A guide to navigating the ceremony with ease.

chapter

6 The Reception   166
Ways to eat, drink, and be merry.

chapter

7 The Perfect Ending   192
Think you're finished? Not quite! Find
out how to wrap up the final details.

chapter

8 Workbook   200
Keep track of your budget, plan your
menu, and more with these easy-to-use
worksheets.

Themes & Ideas   209
Dozens of great theme and project ideas
from the For Better or For Worse wedding
professionals.

chapter

9 Projects   225
Money-saving projects you can create
with ease!

Index   252

Resources   256

Meet the

Meet the

An introduction to the host and wedding

Experts

planners of For Better or For Worse.

On every episode of TLC's For Better or For Worse one wedding planner is given $5,000, a week, and a team of family and friends of the bride and groom to create a memorable event. Here's your opportunity to meet the planners who make it all happen, as well as the host who does everything from helping with the preparations to calming the nervous couple during the days leading up to the surprise ceremony and reception.

Throughout this book you will find dozens of money-saving tips and tricks from these talented wedding-planning professionals. And, as an added bonus, you can see some of the memorable events they have planned (beginning on page 209) and instructions for many of the great projects they have created (see page 225).

If you are interested in having one of the For Better or For Worse wedding planners make your wedding-day dreams come true, turn to the Resources on page 256 for contact information.

Alecia Davis

As the engaging host of TLC's **For Better or For Worse,** Alecia Davis guides couples through the "I dos" and "I don'ts" of planning a wedding. Her easygoing personality is perfect for the job of seeing couples through their jitters, and it's a role she doesn't take lightly. "There is something special about being a part of a couple's wedding day," Alecia says. "This is one of the biggest days of their lives, and I'm invited to help make it something wonderful."

Before turning her attention to weddings, this self-professed former tomboy and athlete traveled the world as a model. Alecia's modeling career, which she put on hold briefly to study broadcast journalism, led her into television hosting. You may recognize her from her red-carpet interviews with celebrities or as host of various country music shows—a perfect fit for this Nashville native.

Alecia, who lives on the West Coast with her miniature Dachshund Rudy, enjoys cooking, traveling, going to movies, and listening to music. She is passionate about childrens' causes and is an active supporter of First Steps, an organization that helps children with special needs. Alecia considers her parents to be her best friends and enjoys visiting them in Nashville, where she can saddle up for some horseback riding.

"My best advice is to just have fun!" "

— Alecia Davis

Alan Dunn

Alan Dunn loves the challenge of making two and two equal five. Whether planning a wrap party for a Hollywood TV show or a wedding for a nervous bride, Alan strives to create the most elegant event imaginable. He's worked with the Hollywood elite, planning numerous weddings, benefits, and parties—including the **Moulin Rouge** Oscar party and various Emmy events.

In addition to his duties on **For Better or For Worse**, Alan is the founder of Tres L.A., a special events and catering company that provides affordable epicurean food. "Don't underestimate the importance of food at any special event," Alan says.

"The best thing you can do if you have a small budget is to make your wedding as intimate as possible. Rather than inviting 200 guests, invite 40 of your closest friends."

— Alan Dunn

Angie Bloom Hewett

Raised in a military family, it's not surprising that Angie Bloom Hewett's approach to planning a wedding is highly organized, involving precision planning with a special emphasis on the details and, of course, style.

Many years of experience in the retail and fashion world have given the former model a savvy sense of style. Her use of flowers, fabrics, colors, and candles helps create beautiful settings. She can make a wedding for 1,200 be a magical and romantic affair that leaves each guest with a sense of inclusion and warmth.

As founder and owner of the wedding firm Moments in Bloom, Angie lends her own personal touch to every event. Her talent for pulling things together to create a unique presentation ensures that the wedding is one of a kind and elegant.

"When planning a wedding, keep in mind that when it's all over you want to remember the day as one of the happiest moments of your life."

— Angie Bloom Hewett

Jackson Lowell

Jackson Lowell is an eclectic creative force! In addition to his wedding planning duties on **For Better or For Worse**, he's a personal stylist to many Hollywood celebrities, as well as a production, costume, and set designer.

Always in demand, Jackson is a regular contributor to many fashion magazines, including **Modern Bride, People**, and **Us**. As a fashion stylist, he worked with Sir Elton John during his 2003 U.S. concert tour, Paula Abdul for the premiere season of **American Idol**, and actor Jimmy Smits when he hosts the 2003 Latin Grammy Awards.

Jackson is also responsible for the look and stunningly unique weddings of various TV and movie stars, including his design of Melissa Joan Hart's spectacular wedding in Florence, Italy.

> **"I love creating an environment. I like the drama of an event."**
>
> — Jackson Lowell

Matt O'Dorisio

With a little design know-how and some flowers, you can make a cave look good, according to Matt O'Dorisio. For Matt, a wedding planner with an extensive design and catering background, the look of the wedding is very important. With a grand theme and ingenuity, Matt transforms the ordinary into the extraordinary.

Since 1999 he has operated his own wedding and events business, Matt O'Dorisio Events. He also freelances as a designer, creating design schemes for high-end residential and commercial interiors.

"When the money is coming out of your own pocket, you tend to get a little more creative."

— Matt O'Dorisio

Erika Shay

It took several twists and turns for Erika Shay to find her true calling as a wedding planner. Erika was raised on a farm near Altoona, Pennsylvania. She attended New York University and graduated as a valedictory representative.

During college Erika landed a job at the Trump Organization working for the Miss Universe pageant. She planned nationally televised events and parties. Erika soon realized weddings were her true passion and incorporated The Princess Bride, a full wedding planning service.

It didn't take long for Erika to realize how much she could do for her brides to alleviate their stress. Aside from wedding planning, Erika also began booking honeymoon travel and became a licensed real estate agent to assist her new couples in finding their dream homes. She currently is making dream weddings come true for her diversified clientele.

"Set a realistic budget based on how much money you actually have, and never, ever, ever expect your gifts to pay for the wedding."

— Erika Shay

Sally Steele

You need nerves of "Steele" to plan a wedding, and Sally lives up to her name where this task is concerned! Since launching Five, her own wedding consulting business in 1999, Sally has planned hundreds of weddings—and she prides herself on remaining calm, cool, and collected during every one. Whether coordinating the details of a wedding for 25 or 1,000, Sally strives to ensure that the big day is festive and stress-free for all in attendance.

In addition to overseeing the day-to-day operations of her own company, Sally is an independent consultant for the Inn of the Seventh Ray in Southern California. Prior to saying "I do" to becoming a wedding planner, Sally worked in catering for several popular restaurants in San Francisco.

"There are hundreds of details to a wedding. As you're planning each detail, you're going to have to draw the line somewhere to keep your budget in line."

— Sally Steele

Getting

From budgeting to prioritizing, here's

Started

how to set your wedding plans in motion.

chapter 1

So you're engaged ... now what? You've pored over the latest bridal magazines and gushed to all your friends. Then it suddenly dawned on you that getting engaged is one thing; pulling off a wedding is another. Where do you start? How do you start?

Whether you're flitting off to tie the knot barefoot on a beach or you're pulling up to the church in a Cinderella-style carriage, getting through the "I dos" involves the same basic strategy. You set priorities, you establish a budget, you come up with a plan, and you execute the plan.

Sound familiar? Perhaps a little like a project at work or the way you track household expenditures? Consider yourself the CEO of a company that's about to embark on the biggest merger of your career. Let the planning begin.

Setting Priorities

Let us be the first to disillusion you: The national average cost for a wedding today is about $20,000. "Everybody gets sticker shock by the cost of a wedding," says wedding planner Alan Dunn. "But things just add up. That's the reality of it. Weddings are expensive."

The good news is that how much your wedding costs is up to you. You may not be able to control the cost of specific items, but you control the spending. Dare we say, you can pull off a wedding to remember for $10,000, $5,000 (as the wedding planners on **For Better or For Worse** do), or even $2,000—the latter if you greatly limit the guest list. "It takes more imagination and creativity, but it's definitely not impossible to have a wedding for under $20,000," wedding planner Matt O'Dorisio says.

It all comes down to priorities. Do you absolutely need that designer gown that no one but you will know is a designer gown? Must you really rent the country club when you're a backyard barbecue kind of couple? Is it necessary to invite people from your parents' dinner club, college friends you lost touch with a decade ago, or coworkers you never speak to unless you have one of those awkward meet-in-the-hallway-alone moments?

Get real! As soon as you start tallying up the costs of all the things you want and all the guests you think you have to invite, you'll rethink things.

"People have champagne tastes on a beer budget; it happens all the time," wedding planner Alan Dunn says. "People have these visions of what they want to do, but they're not realistic. The reality is that there are going to be compromises. You have to figure out what's important to you and go with that."

Start with the big stuff: Are you willing to delay major purchases—a house, a new car, laser-eye surgery—in exchange for your wedding? If not, you'll need to keep your wedding small and simple. Then move on to the wedding itself. Perhaps you'd rather splurge on a once-in-a-lifetime trip than on the wedding, so you're both fine with getting hitched at the courthouse. Maybe you want to nix the DJ or band at your reception for fear that your two left feet will take over. Talking through goals and setting priorities is not just a wakeup call for your wallet; it also helps put your relationship on sounder footing in terms of communication, something that will be key throughout your married life.

Block off an hour of quiet time so the two of you can discuss general thoughts on the type of wedding you envision. Weddings come in many forms, from simple ceremonies set in parks to regal galas in cathedrals, and the price tag adjusts accordingly. You'll waste time and probably some money if one of you is booking a flight to Vegas to tie the knot in an all-night chapel while the other is scoping out the largest, grandest venue in town.

Without getting hung up on the details (we'll cover those later), come to a meeting of the minds on some general areas. Remember that more this and more that means more money. To jump-start the conversation, consider these topics:

Date. Choosing a date for your wedding is one of the first considerations. Unless there's a compelling reason to do so, don't get locked into one date at this time. Choosing several possible dates will give you flexibility and possible cost savings when you look for venues.

Size. The number of guests you invite to your wedding will obviously affect your budget, but there's more to it than dollar signs. What's your comfort level and personality? Are you more at ease in small-group settings? Do you love or hate being the center of attention? Do you want an intimate wedding with family and close friends, or do you long for a guest list big enough to fill a stadium? Do you have a big brood of relatives or a large circle of friends to invite? Your answers to these questions will help you determine the size of your guest list.

Mutual Decisions

You may be surprised to discover what your mate's priorities are—and what they aren't. Fill in the blanks to help determine where to spend your wedding dollars. Refer back to this list to resist the temptation to splurge on things in the "can do without" column—such as a flutist at the wedding ceremony or fresh shrimp at the reception. And remember: This is a starting point. If you don't have the money, you'll need to move some of the "gotta haves" into another column.

Gotta Have	Would Like to Have	Can Do Without

Location. What's your ideal wedding site? In a church, synagogue, or other house of worship? Outdoors? A tropical locale? At the courthouse? How about the reception site? The desired sites will affect your guest list and the overall bottom line.

Ambiance. Do you want things fancy or casual? Do you envision guests carefreely mingling or properly placed at tables for a sit-down meal? A casual wedding generally costs less than a formal one, but a fancy affair can be done on a small budget if you get creative and whittle the guest list. You probably already have a mental picture of what you want your wedding and reception to look and feel like; use that as a guide.

Pet peeves or must-haves. There are probably certain things about weddings you've attended that you either loved or loathed. Get them out in the open early on. Maybe you think having seven attendants on each side is overload or having a cash bar is chintzy. Maybe you attended a potluck-style reception and you want to bring that idea to your own reception. Speak now, or forever hold your peace.

After mulling your general ideas, get specific. Grab a sheet of paper, and make a list of your top five priorities. There are no rights or wrongs about what makes the list. If you both love to cook, food may be at the top of the list. If you couldn't care less about attire, a gown and tux may not even make your top five list. Use the priority list to stay focused on the things that are most important to you, and therefore deserve the biggest chunks of your budget. You'll quickly find out that it all comes back to money. If you or a relative haven't hit the jackpot lately, be prepared to let money, not fantasy, drive your ultimate decisions. You can't serve caviar on a meat-and-cheese-platter budget—at least not if you want to invite 200 guests. But if you really want caviar—say if food is at the top of your list—you can cut the guest list to 50 to make it happen. That's where the importance of setting priorities comes in.

Money Matters

If your impending nuptials are sparking more questions in your mind about dress styles and wild bachelor parties than money, it's time to get a grip on reality. Finances aren't the sexiest part of planning a wedding, but if they're tossed aside like a big-bowed bridesmaid's dress, they can ruin your happily ever after. No one wants to start a marriage with maxed-out credit cards and an empty savings account from frivolous spending. Nor do you want to waltz down the aisle with a pit in your stomach because you know you've overspent on the dress or tux you're wearing, the bows on the pews, and the floral arrangements on the altar.

The main thing to remember about money is simple: It doesn't grow on trees. (Ah, but wouldn't it be nice if you could just tell the florist to pluck a $1,000 bill from the big old oak out back?) Figuring out how to get the wedding you want and can afford is a chicken-or-the-egg question. Should you set a budget first and work from there? Or should you start tallying up the cost

Expert Advice To figure out what your priorities are, wedding planner Jackson Lowell recommends grabbing some note cards and a marker, and then writing a key wedding element, such as "Cake," "Photos," "Food," or "Wedding Dress," on each card. Spread the cards out on a table and move them around until you both agree on an order of importance. Write down the order on a sheet of paper, and your priority list is done.

of your priorities and dive into the details of your dream wedding? We suggest starting somewhere in the middle.

As soon as you've set your priorities, have a serious talk about where the money will come from. Brace yourself if you think the bride's parents are eagerly waiting in the wings to foot most of the bill. There are no hard, fast rules anymore about who pays for what. "It's a very modern world," wedding planner Sally Steele says. "Who pays for what is very open." Potential sources for your money tree include the following:

You and yours. Today's brides and grooms are shouldering a fair share, sometimes all, of the wedding expenses. The talk we suggested earlier about setting your big priorities (Do you want to save money for a house, car, laser-eye surgery?) will help you focus your funds. If you want the $20,000 that's sitting in your bank account for a down payment on a house or that once-in-a-lifetime trip, it's off-limits for your wedding. So what does that leave you? If it's $2,000, you need to start planning for a supersmall wedding or a big boost from the parents. You might be able to rustle up a few thousand dollars by holding a garage sale, selling the treadmill you never use, or moonlighting at a fast-food joint. "When the money is coming out of your own pocket, you tend to get a little more creative," Matt O'Dorisio says.

Parents. Divvying up the bills used to be cut-and-dried: The bride's family paid for the wedding, and the groom's family paid for the rehearsal dinner. That tradition has gone the way of veil-covered faces and white-only bridal gowns. Blended families have thrown conventional wedding rules for a loop. Do you dare ask a stepparent to foot part of the bill? Talk to both—make that all—sides of the family to determine what, if anything, they can pay for. Don't sound greedy or entitled. Explain that you're putting together a budget, and as such you're tallying up all revenue sources to come up with a realistic amount. Before you do, though, read "Who Does What?" on page 49. If you know your parents are strapped for money, don't put them on the spot. To ease their worries about how they can afford to help, let them know that you and your spouse-to-be have the money saved to pay for the wedding.

The Money Tree

Eliminate guesswork and last-minute surprises by getting pertinent parties on board about bills.

Bride will pay for:

_____
_____
_____

Groom will pay for:

_____
_____
_____

Bride's parents/stepparents will pay for:

_____
_____
_____

Groom's parents/stepparents will pay for:

_____
_____
_____

Other potential sources of income
(from other relatives, garage sale, etc.):

_____
_____
_____

Gifts. So you've hatched a great plan where you return all the gifts or use the money guests give you to pay for your shindig? Get that thought out of your mind right now. If you're lucky the monetary gifts will cover the cost of the cake or maybe the food. Sadly some couples do bank on the gifts to get them out of debt, and they discover after the fact that it didn't work out. This is a foolish way to budget—and is an absolute no-no.

The Budget

There are a couple approaches to making a budget. You can tally up the amount you and your families can contribute and work within that lump sum. Or you can estimate the cost of individual items to determine how much your dream wedding—or at least a wedding you're comfortable paying for—would cost, and then begin whittling down from there. The latter may mean using your noggin to make it happen: borrowing a bridal gown from a friend, convincing your uncle to let you use his clubhouse membership for the reception, or selling the extra set of furniture to cover some expenses.

Whatever approach you choose, itemizing is key to keeping you on track and pinpointing trouble spots. Use the budget worksheet in Chapter 8, page 202, to help you develop a budget. If desired transfer the information to a computer software program to keep track of things electronically.

Your budget may look all well and good on paper, but then along comes a flood of bills. Instead of waiting for them to roll in, figure out a payment method as you're hammering out a budget. Will it be cash, check, or charge—maybe with a little begging and borrowing mixed in?

Cash is impractical for obvious reasons: You'd have to carry a big wad around with you to plunk down deposits and pay for expenses. However, if you need discipline, paying by cash might be a novel visual cue to keep you within your budget. Borrowing—at least in the form of taking out a bank loan—should be off your radar too. Begging is doable, at least for the brief time your parents—or your guardian angel—are willing to put up with it. If your parents do commit to chipping in some money, find out when and how that will be done. Will they write you a check to use at your own discretion, or do they plan to directly pay for a specific expense, such as the bride's outfit or the rehearsal dinner? (continued on page 28)

Test Your Spending Habits

Take this quiz to get an idea of your own and your mate's spending and saving habits. The answers will reveal things that will come in handy when budgeting for your wedding.

1 True/False. You know the price of a gallon of milk within a few pennies.

What do milk prices have to do with weddings, you may wonder? If you're in-the-know about the average cost of a gallon of milk, you're probably attuned to how much you're spending on specific items on a daily basis, and it will come easily to you while working out the budget details of the wedding. If you're not, you may need to get a better handle on the challenges of planning and paying for the big day.

2 When it's time to pay the rent or mortgage each month, does your spouse-to-be

a) write a check two weeks before it's due and record the transaction in his/her check register?
b) dash off a check the day it's due and later wonder if the bill was paid on time?
c) mail the payment four days late, including extra for the late fee?

d) rely on a roommate, parents, or you to take care of matters?

If you don't already know the answer to this question, find out—fast! The way your mate handles an important regular bill is a good indication of how he or she will deal with wedding expenses.

3 True/False. Borrowing money for a wedding is considered "good debt" like student loans and mortgages.

False. "Good debt" is a liability with an asset or investment that goes along with it. A mortgage is an investment in a home and the land it stands on. A student loan is an investment in your potential earning power. On the flip side, a wedding (financially speaking) is similar to having credit card debt.

4 You find a designer suit that fits you perfectly, but you know a store on the other side of town has an off-brand replica for a quarter of the price. Which suit do you buy?

Despite an occasional splurge, if you're not too label-conscious or brand-loyal you'll have an easier time passing up high-priced wedding fare for just-as-stylish bargain options.

5 True/False. You know exactly how much debt your mate has.

Be honest here. If he or she knows about the balance on your student loan, but not the hefty sum due on your credit card, it's time to have a chat. A wedding is often the first big expense a couple will encounter together, and you should both be comfortable talking about large sums of money and debt. It's a good way to work as a team while planning your event and it will create a precedent for your new life together.

6 When you plan a romantic evening, you

a) pick up takeout from your favorite fast-food restaurant and later take a leisurely walk in the twilight together.
b) head over to one of your parents' homes for a home-cooked meal and to spend quality time with your family.
c) go out to dinner and then to a movie to see the latest romantic comedy.

d) put on your best outfit and spend an upscale evening complete with dinner and dancing.

These are all great options, but some are pricier than others. Your idea of the perfect date can help you narrow down what's important to you about your wedding day. You don't have to re-create the entire experience, just pick the most important element of the evening and find a way to include it in your wedding budget. In the end you'll have the feel of a great date in your special celebration.

7 When you close your eyes and think about your wedding, the image that first comes to mind is

a) a fantasy gown.
b) where to hang the framed photo of the two of you.
c) sharing the first dance with your new spouse.
d) family and friends casually frolicking in a park.

If you're having trouble deciding how much to spend on certain items for your big day, your daydreams can offer a clue to what you feel is most important. You may feel comfortable splurging on a special item while scaling back on other elements.

That leaves check or charge as your options. Often you'll want both. Open a joint account earmarked exclusively for your wedding expenses; deposit the funds you've pulled together into the checking account. If you're planning an out-of-town wedding or doing a lot of online shopping, a credit card is virtually a requirement. Strive to pay the full amount due each month to avoid costly finance charges.

Forgotten Expenses

Unless you're a CPA who knows where every penny is going, you'll find that it's easy for your budget to get out of whack. The $500 worth of flowers you ordered may end up being more like $550 when taxes and delivery charges are included. The smartest thing, obviously, is to factor in every charge up front, or at least before placing an order. Because that may not always happen, it's a good idea to set up a small slush fund for things you may not have thought about, such as the following (and see Chapter 3, page 77, for precautions on hidden costs):

Gratuities. Anyone who travels frequently doesn't leave home without a wad of dollar bills for bellhops, airport attendants, cab drivers, and others. You'll encounter similar situations with your wedding vendors. Be prepared to tip and tip often (see "Tip Sheet" **opposite**). Be sure to check contracts with vendors to see if the gratuity is already included so you don't end up tipping twice. For vendors you've worked closely with and other special helpers, a small gift, rather than money, is a nice way to personalize your gratitude. Be sure to budget for those too. Even a few batches of cookies and decorative bags to wrap them in adds up.

Deposits. The money you fork over to secure a site or order attire is usually applied to the overall cost. On occasion a vendor may cry foul and keep the deposit money (say, if your crazed guests break every champagne glass in the place or the bridal salon goes belly-up before your dress arrives). Short of a lawsuit, you usually can't do much to get a deposit returned. Be sure you read the fine print on contracts so you know the terms of deposit money, including any conditions for which it won't be returned or applied to the final payment.

Licenses and permits. Depending on the sites you choose and type of wedding you're having, you may end up paying fees. Don't assume the botanical garden that's open to the public is free. Even if it is, it may require a special permit from the city. You may also end up paying for such things as parking permits (residents may not appreciate you roping off a street near the park where you're exchanging vows) and a liquor license if the establishment you're using doesn't already have one. And don't forget the most important document of all: the marriage license and, depending upon your state, blood tests. (See Chapter 3, page 121, for more about legal details.)

The extras. Remember to factor in things such as sales tax, delivery charges, and shipping and handling costs to your purchases. The $500 dress you order online will end up being more once it's in your virtual shopping cart and the shipping is factored in. Alterations will run up the tab even more. A few extra bucks here and there can quickly add up. Rush charges are even worse—they can double the price of an item—so avoid them at all cost.

Tip Sheet

Use these guidelines to determine what to tip vendors who have provided great service. If in doubt about how much to tip, fall back on the general 10 to 20 percent rule. If friends or relatives are doing the duties, a small gift or a big thank you is more appropriate.

- **Band/DJ:** $25 or more per person
- **Bartenders:** $25 or more per person
- **Delivery person:** $10 (more if the person stays for setup)
- **Hair stylist/makeup artist:** 10 to 20 percent of the total bill
- **Officiant:** $50 or more (a tip, per se, is not given, but an honorarium or donation is)
- **Photographer:** $50 or more (often only given for above-and-beyond)

The Wedding Planner

You read that right. This section is about wedding planners. You may be wondering what it's doing in a book with "cost-conscious" in its title. After all, aren't wedding planners reserved for your snobby, rich acquaintances?

Here's the scoop: Hiring a wedding planner does cost money. Some planners charge an hourly fee; others charge a percentage of the overall tab, anywhere between 10 and 20 percent. With the national average for a wedding today costing about $20,000 that adds up to a big chunk of change. (Don't worry, we're not suggesting that you have to spend $20,000—or even close to that—to have a great wedding. It all goes back to priorities.) So how is it that a growing number of average Joes and Janes are able to afford wedding planners? Maybe they just hired the person for the day. For about $500 you can probably hire a wedding coordinator to keep the ceremony and reception running smoothly—a smart investment for an anxious bride or groom. Maybe the couples made a wedding planner their top priority, so they were willing to forgo the designer gown, fancy appetizers, and hot-air balloon rides.

Whether a wedding planner actually saves you money in the long run is open for debate. It's true that a well-connected planner can get deals on venues, flowers, and caterers. How much of an impact that makes on your bottom line

Quick Tip

Less is less when it comes to keeping your budget in line. Typically the less formal the wedding, the less costly it is. The fewer guests you invite, the fewer expenses you'll have. The less traditional your reception site (think barn out in the country), the less your fee will be. Get the picture?

depends on the individual circumstances. Wedding planner Jackson Lowell doesn't sugarcoat it. "It's a misconception that I'm going to save [you] thousands of dollars," he says. "What I am going to do is give you access to vendors you wouldn't necessarily have and options that you would be floundering to find on your own. Vendors will give me things they wouldn't give you, but it's not going to save you thousands of dollars." For example, a wedding planner might be able to rent chairs for $7 each rather than $12.

What a wedding planner will save you is time. The planner does the legwork, and you say yea or nay. A wedding planner is skilled at reading contracts, including determining what is and isn't included, and in planning the logistics of the ceremony and reception. Wedding planner Angie Bloom Hewett also sees her role as peacekeeper—someone who helps the bride stay composed during what is usually an emotionally charged time and who can meet her expectations. "A bride can go into a divadom place and not always be lovable," Angie says. "This is the one time for her to be walking on the red carpet, so to speak. We grow up with Cinderella, Snow White, and all the fairy tales, so when it's her time, she just wants it to be right. There can be such high expectations."

Indeed some brides have played out all the details of their wedding since they were little girls. The details may be etched in their mind, so they don't need a planner—or maybe it's so etched in their mind that they need an expert to pull it off exactly as they envision. While you're knee-deep in budgeting, ask yourself these questions before crossing a wedding planner off your list:

What's your time worth? Remember that time is money. If you're eating up all your vacation—or (cough, cough) sick days—on wedding errands, you might decide that it's better to let someone else do the work. If you're a computer consultant who charges $80 an hour, are you willing to pass up jobs when you might be able to find a $40 an hour planner? If you simply find planning overwhelming and can't get your work and household chores done, you may decide you're willing to give up a few of the "extras" in your budget to hire a planner or at least a coordinator for the day of the wedding.

(continued on page 36)

For Better **Your budget allows the luxury of a wedding planner to coordinate logistics, deal with vendors, and basically make your life easier.**

For Worse **So you don't have funds for a wedding planner. Don't fret. Just think like a planner. Set up a grab-and-go organizational system that includes a binder-style organizer to stash pages you've ripped from magazines, business cards from potential vendors, and paper for jotting down notes. Getting and staying organized is key.**

Ask the Wedding Planner

If you are considering a wedding planner, use the answers to these questions to determine whether you have found a good match for your budget and personalities.

• How do you charge? By the hour? Flat fee? Percentage of overall costs (and, if so, how is that figured)?

• Are you available on our wedding day? Does our time frame fit with your schedule and comfort level?

• Do you have other weddings you'll be working on simultaneously? How many weddings do you typically work on at the same time?

• Is this your full-time job? Do you do weddings exclusively or do you plan other events?

• Are you a full-service planner, or can we select certain areas in which we'd like your assistance? Could we hire you for the day of the wedding only, if desired?

• Are there certain things you won't do?

• How do you bill? How often do you expect payment?

• Will you have a contract for us to sign that details what is included in the fee?

• Do you work on your own? Do you have a staff or hire workers on an as-needed basis?

• How long have you been in business? How many weddings have you planned in the past year? Past five years?

• What's the typical budget of weddings you've planned? What was the largest budget? What was the smallest budget?

• Can you work with our budget? Do you see it as a challenge?

• What's your ideal time frame for planning a wedding? What's the fastest you've had to pull a wedding together?

• How frequently will you be in contact with us, or can we be in contact with you?

• What's your specialty or area of expertise? What sets you apart from other planners?

• What's your style?

• What trends have you noticed with weddings/receptions?

• Are you affiliated with any wedding-planner organizations?

• Do you get a commission from vendors you recommend?

• Do you attend the actual ceremony and reception?

• What would happen if we needed to cancel? Is there a cancellation fee?

• Can we see your portfolio?

• Can we get references from recent clients?

Spend or Save?

We asked the six wedding planners from For Better or For Worse **to chime in on the following areas, and we tallied up the answers to give you some insight. In most cases there wasn't a consensus—which proves how important it is to set priorities and focus your funds on areas that are most important to you.**

Bridal Gown

$Save$ Sorry brides! There's no reason to let a dress you'll only wear once suck up your budget. You can find drop-dead gorgeous gowns for a fraction of the price of designer fare. You can borrow or beg (most bridal salons expect some dickering). Unless all your guests are fashionistas, no one will know or care whose name is on the label.

Cake

$Save$ Chalk it up to planners who have seen too many gorgeous cakes that tasted horrible. Beauty is only skin deep, even with cake. Go for taste, not the pricey extras on the exterior. "There's no reason why the cake has to cost more than a couple hundred bucks," says wedding planner Matt O'Dorisio. An exception: If you're having a cake and champagne reception, splurge on the confection.

Photography

$Spend$ No gray area here: All six planners agree that photography should be a splurge (staying within your means, of course). Entrusting the photography to a novice or a cheap, bad photographer is "like building a beautiful house on no foundation," says wedding planner Angie Bloom Hewett.

Videography

$Save$ If your budget is tight, the decision is made for you. You won't have the bucks to hire a professional videographer, which can cost thousands of dollars. (If money isn't an issue, go for it.) For the cost-conscious, have a friend or relative tape the event, and then brace yourself for a seasick sensation as you watch.

Flowers

$Save$ No one will argue that flowers look great; the problem is that the costs can get out of control. By all means bring in flowers, but find creative ways to keep the costs down. "Flowers are beautiful; one flower is also beautiful," wedding planner Sally Steele says. The emphasis here is on one striking and simple flower: bridesmaids carrying a single rose, a lone orchid as the centerpiece on a table.

Wedding Ceremony Decorations

Depends This one was all over the board: The For Better or For Worse wedding planners have different opinions on how much to spend on decorations. The bottom line is that the ceremony site should look nice. If you choose your location wisely— a garden in bloom, a church with a beautiful altar, a mountainside setting—you can skimp. If the venue is unattractive you'll need to spruce it up.

Reception Decorations

Save Three words come into play on this: recycle, recycle, recycle. The floral arrangements, bouquets, candles, and other pretties used at the wedding ceremony should reappear at the reception site. If you didn't have any of those elements at the ceremony, candles are an inexpensive decoration.

Food

Spend The food is your gift to guests, so plan to go the extra mile to get the tastiest food your budget can buy. Wedding planner Alan Dunn is such a foodie that he'd rather cut the guest list than serve lackluster eats.

Reception Music

Spend If you're having music, have music. Don't skimp by having your teenage neighbor blast tunes from a boom box. "The music is a big part of how much fun people have at the reception," says wedding planner Erika Shay. "The band or DJ you pick to play the music is really controlling how many people are going to be up on their feet dancing and how good of a time they have."

Transportation

Save Skip the limo and have a friend or relative chauffeur you from the ceremony site to the reception. If you insist on renting, a luxury sedan from a car rental agency is usually cheaper than a limo service, which jacks up its prices at the mere mention of wedding bells. An exception: If the transportation is something integral to the ambiance of your day, say carting guests to and from the sites in horse-drawn wagons, you may decide it's worth a splurge.

What's your expertise? Are you a decorating diva or a galloping gourmet? You may not need outside help to plan decorations or menus—unless, say, your negotiation skills are as suave as a used-car salesperson's. Assess your strengths and weaknesses as a couple. If you both lack in certain areas, you might want to look for a wedding planner to handle those portions. You'll need to look for someone who isn't solely a full-service planner.

What's the time frame? If it's just not humanly possible to pull off the type of wedding you want on the time frame you have, a wedding planner may be your saving grace. Sometimes your situation may demand such a service. If you're planning a wedding in another city or a faraway locale, hiring a local planner can save you a lot of headache—and long-distance phone bills.

What's your overall budget? You've got to be realistic. If your total budget is $3,000, you're probably not going to find a full-service planner who's willing to work on a percentage basis. His or her commission would just be too small to justify the time. And if you paid the person hourly, you'd probably eat up your entire budget on just that. You can still look into hiring someone for the day of the wedding, but that too will take hundreds of dollars. That said, don't be shy about calling a planner whose work you admire. "Most of us do this because we love weddings," says wedding planner Erika Shay. If nothing else, that planner may be able to hook you up with one of his or her assistants or someone else, she says.

All this begs the question: Where do you find a wedding planner? Ask friends, call bridal salons, check your phone book, and search the Internet for professional organizations, such as the Association of Professional Bridal Consultants, whose membership consists of wedding planners across the country. Another option is to consider people who are professional party or special-events planners. They have skills in finding sites, dealing with caterers, and coming up with creative decorations.

The Guest List

uests ... already? Yep! If you thought you could delay compiling the guest list until just before the invitations go out, think again. The guest list drives so many things. You can't book venues until you know how many people will be there, you can't decide on a menu until you know how many mouths you have to feed, and so forth.

The equation is simple: More guests equal more everything. It means more invitations (and more time spent digging up addresses), more space, more seating, more tables to decorate, more food at the reception. In short, it means more money. The guest list itself can get the best-planned budget out of whack. If a five-course gourmet meal is at the top of your priority list, there's a good chance you'll need to limit guests to 50 rather than 250 so you can afford your top priority. If you're determined to send every guest home with a slice of cake packaged in a pretty little box, you'll pay less if the list is short. The guest list can also help you with venue selections. If you know you have 150 guests, it automatically rules out holding the ceremony in the quaint little church that seats 25. And why book a venue that holds 500 people when you end up inviting only 100? You've just thrown money down the drain. All of this, and more, is why the guest list is so critical.

"Make the guest list right after you get engaged, and every day keep cutting it down," wedding planner Erika Shay says. "Sit down and really keep chopping the list down, down, down." (continued on page 41)

Timeline Checklist

This list will help keep you on track time-wise. Fill in the target date for completion of each phase. If the time frame noted doesn't work with you, put your planning on fast-forward. Cross out items that don't pertain to your wedding, and use the blank lines to write in other tasks.

Phase 1 (Ideally done 9 to 12 months before wedding)

☐ Announce engagement to family and friends.

☐ Discuss priorities, such as the type, size, and formality of wedding and reception.

☐ Make a list of your top five or top ten priorities, which will guide all spending decisions.

☐ Discuss finances, including if and what family members will contribute.

☐ Establish a budget.

☐ Open joint checking account and/or credit card.

☐ Select wedding date and alternative dates.

☐ Get a rough (but good) idea of guest list.

☐ Discuss and visit possible ceremony and reception locations.

☐ Set up organizational system (such as a binder or computer spreadsheets).

☐ Look through magazines and search online to get ideas on attire, invitations, flowers, cake, and so forth.

☐ Hire a wedding planner.

☐ Finalize the wedding date.

☐ Book a ceremony site.

☐ Book a reception site.

_____

_____

Target Date for Completion: _____

Phase 2 (Ideally done 6 to 8 months before wedding)

☐ Find out requirements for marriage license and other legal issues.

☐ Select and ask attendants and other special helpers, such as a guest-book attendant, to take part in your wedding.

☐ Select invitations and other stationery items, such as thank-you cards.

☐ Mail or e-mail "save the date" cards.

☐ Announce engagement in newspaper(s).

☐ Register for gifts at store(s) and/or online.

☐ Begin shopping for (or making a plan to do it yourself) attire, photographer, caterer, baker, florist, and wedding bands.

☐ Determine what tasks you need help with, such as decorating the venues or picking up flowers, and assign friends and relatives to them.

☐ Order, or have someone begin making, bridal attire.

- ☐ Book a photographer.
- ☐ Book a caterer.
- ☐ Book a baker.
- ☐ Book a florist.
- ☐ Book a band, DJ, or other entertainment for reception.
- ☐ Check budget to make sure you're not overspending.

Target Date for Completion:_____

Phase 3 (Ideally done 4 to 5 months before wedding)

- ☐ Select and order men's attire.
- ☐ Finalize guest list.
- ☐ Choose and meet with officiant and schedule any required premarital classes.
- ☐ Select musicians for ceremony.
- ☐ Select music for ceremony.
- ☐ Purchase or make decorations.
- ☐ Reserve a block of hotel rooms for guests.
- ☐ Make honeymoon plans.
- ☐ Check budget to make sure you're not overspending.

_____

_____

Target Date for Completion:_____

Phase 4 (Ideally done 1 to 3 months before wedding)

- ☐ Mail invitations.
- ☐ Finalize photography needs.

- ☐ Finalize menu.
- ☐ Finalize cake/dessert.
- ☐ Finalize flowers.
- ☐ Purchase or make favors.
- ☐ Purchase or make gifts for attendants and other special helpers.
- ☐ Purchase or make gift to bride or groom.
- ☐ Make arrangements for rehearsal, including dinner.
- ☐ Invite people to rehearsal and dinner.
- ☐ Arrange wedding-day transportation between venues; book any rental or service.
- ☐ Finalize ceremony details, including vows and program.
- ☐ Purchase or order wedding bands.
- ☐ Review and update gift registry.
- ☐ Pick up bridal attire; schedule alterations.
- ☐ Schedule appointments with hair stylist and other beauty-related services.
- ☐ Begin writing thank-you notes for gifts that have been received.
- ☐ Check budget to make sure you're not overspending.

_____

_____

Target Date for Completion:_____

(continued)

Timeline Checklist (continued)

Phase 5 (Ideally done 2 to 3 weeks before wedding)

☐ Get marriage license and finalize other legal matters.

☐ Finalize honeymoon plans.

☐ Make and distribute wedding-day itinerary to attendants, family, and other helpers.

☐ Attend bachelor/bachelorette parties.

☐ Continue writing thank-you notes for gifts that have been received.

☐ Check your budget to make sure you're not overspending.

_____

_____

Target Date for Completion:_____

Phase 6 (1 week before to day before wedding)

☐ Confirm that you're on all vendors' schedules, as well as that of friends and family in charge of various wedding-day tasks.

☐ Give final head count to caterer and determine seating chart.

☐ Pick up any rental attire.

☐ Pack wedding-day bag, including accessories and "emergency" items such as safety pins.

☐ Pack honeymoon bags.

☐ Attend rehearsal and dinner.

☐ Go to beauty-related appointments.

☐ Run through last-minute details.

☐ Check budget to make sure you're not overspending.

_____

_____

Target Date for Completion:_____

Phase 7 (Day of Wedding)

☐ Go to hair stylist.

☐ Eat.

☐ Take wedding-day bag and attire to ceremony site.

☐ Take a deep breath and relax!

Phase 8 (Post-wedding)

☐ Return rental attire.

☐ Send thank-you notes to attendants and special helpers.

☐ Open gifts.

☐ Complete all thank-you notes for gifts received.

☐ Have dress dry-cleaned.

☐ Pay bills.

☐ Balance budget.

Target Date for Completion:_____

To keep the list from becoming a litany of names you don't recognize, with parents and siblings e-mailing or phoning daily with more people to invite, Erika prefers hashing things out in person, if possible. Get key players together, including parents, and hammer out the initial list, she says.

If desired, set up categories, such as "Must Invite," "Should Invite," and "Invite If Possible." This provides a starting point and makes it easier to tweak the list down the road. Though you should have more than a ballpark estimate, especially if you're ready to book a venue, you can fine-tune the list later—the stipulation being that there can be no big jumps in the number of people added to or taken off the list.

Setting some boundaries will help take the guesswork out of the task and alleviate possible family feuds. One guideline some wedding planners suggest is that the bride or groom should be able to recognize every face when they walk down the aisle or stand at the altar. If they're seeing a sea of strangers, it's a sign Mom, Dad, or someone else had too much input in compiling the guest list. Consider these points too:

Who's making the cut? Establish any cut-off points, such as no children, no coworkers, no former boyfriends or girlfriends, no third cousins, and so forth. You'll need to talk this through as a couple, as well as with immediate family members. (continued on page 44)

Expert Advice **Don't have a fallback guest list, where you invite someone new if someone on your A list can't make it. "If you have someone on a B list, they're not a close enough friend to be at your wedding," wedding planner Erika Shay says. "Why bother? Save your money."**

A Family Affair

Balancing family and friends as you plan your big day can be tricky. Use this quiz to help you wade through murky waters and understand how budget affects some of these decisions.

1 Your great-aunt Bertha has always been close to your family, spending holidays and vacations with you. You want to ask her to be a part of the wedding. It's most appropriate to ask her to

a) be the guest-book attendant.
b) make the wedding cake.
c) be your matron of honor.
d) officiate.

Any of the above. It's perfectly acceptable to ask people to fill any role in your wedding day, regardless of their relationship to you or their age. The possibilities are endless and give you the opportunity to honor a friend or family member by asking him or her to have a hand in your celebration. Try to match up people's talents and interests with the roles you have to fill. If great-aunt Bertha is terrified of speaking in public, but is an excellent pianist, for example, ask her to play for the ceremony rather than officiate.

2 True/False. The bride's parents/stepparents are expected to foot the bill for the ceremony, and the groom's parents/stepparents pay for the rehearsal dinner.

False. While this might have been the rule in the '50s, times have changed. It's more common these days for the bride and groom to pay for a portion or all of the wedding. Their parents may pitch in a certain amount to the pot to be spent as the couple sees fit or to agree to pay for a certain element for the day, such as the flowers.

3 You have a young niece and nephew who are just the right age to be in the wedding party, but you've planned a simple ceremony with only two attendants. Do you have to offer them spots in the wedding party to help them feel like a part of your celebration?

No. If having children in the wedding party doesn't fit in with your vision of the day, there are other ways of involving them. Ask them to help hand out programs, give them honorary "attendant" titles and have them wear a small corsage or boutonniere (a little sprig of flowers goes a long way!), or promise to dance with them to a song they pick out at the reception.

4 True/False. You have six close friends from college. Because they're planning on coming to the wedding regardless, asking them all to be attendants won't affect the budget's bottom line.

False. Although they won't be adding to the reception head count (they'll be there either way), asking all six to be a part of the ceremony will raise the final total. You'll be adding to the bill for the rehearsal dinner, special attendant gifts, bouquets or boutonnieres, and photography time. If you want to include them as a group in the celebration, consider asking them to handle another job together, such as serving cake or tending the bar for an hour.

5 True/False. Your parents are divorced and aren't on the best terms, but they should still be seated next to each other during the ceremony.

False. Just because it's your big day, don't assume your divorced parents will be chummy with one another. Give them some breathing room—especially if one parent has remarried. Seat a sibling or two between them, or have the mother sit in the front row (ladies first!) and the father in the second row.

6 True/False. You were an attendant in your cousin's wedding a decade ago, so now you have to reciprocate.

False. Wedding parties aren't like good deeds: One doesn't necessarily deserve another. You should ask people to be your attendants because you're close to them and want them standing next to you as you leap into matrimony—not because you feel obligated. This is one way wedding budgets can balloon out of control. You can always ask the person to play a smaller role in the celebration.

7 True/False. A bride can have a male "bridesmaid," and a groom can have a female "groomsman."

True. Women have close male friends, and men have close female friends. There's no reason to ask them to sit and watch when there isn't anyone else you'd rather have by your side. Change the titles to generic "attendant," rather than specifying bridesmaid and groomsman; use the term "honor attendant" for a male "maid of honor" or a female "best man." And no, a groom's female friend doesn't have to wear a tux to stand on his side, and a bride's male friend doesn't have to wear a dress (unless, of course, they want to!). Dress all the men in the wedding party in the same attire, and all the women in the same attire, regardless of which side they'll be standing on.

Parental controls. If parents are footing a big chunk of the bill, it stands to reason that they should have some say in who's invited. Make sure they're aware of the boundaries you and your spouse-to-be have agreed upon, but grant them some leeway in inviting their own guests. This is where the art of persuasion and compromise comes in. Avoid giving them a magic number, such as letting them invite 20 guests. They may only have 10 people they really want to invite, but because you've offered up 20 they'll pad their list.

Gut instinct. Try as you might, there's no scientific way to form a guest list. Your gut instinct is often your best guide. You know who's special to you and would be happy to be a part of your big day.

Establishing a Timeline

Conventional wisdom—the emphasis being on "conventional"—says to allot one year to plan a wedding. Who's kidding whom? Many couples today don't have the luxury of time, or simply don't want to drag things out after popping the question. Case in point: The **For Better or For Worse** wedding planners have a week to plan and pull off an affair to remember for a lucky bride and groom.

Whether you're planning a quickie wedding or a lengthy engagement, you'll need to budget your time wisely. (And you thought you were done with budgets?) Your money isn't the only thing that's valuable. To keep the stress in check during the hustle-bustle, consider these time-management tips:

Take baby steps. In the workforce how many times have you heard someone say to look at the big picture? Well this is one time when thinking small may save your sanity. Looking at everything that you have to accomplish before the big day can be overwhelming, so break tasks into smaller, more manageable chunks. The "Timeline Checklist" on page 38 will get you going. Granted, if you only have two weeks to plan a wedding, you'll have to fast-forward things and take leaps, rather than small steps.

Delegate. One person can't do it all—nor should he or she have to. Have a chat with your mate to divvy up tasks. Don't stop there. Enlist the help of family members and friends, taking advantage of their special talents. An aunt who loves to bake might enjoy calling bakeries to get estimates and photos of their work, or a friend who's a graphic designer may have ideas for your wedding program and might even volunteer to make them.

Get organized. You probably know that panicked feeling of hunting for keys when you're already late for work or searching through piles on your desk to try to find an important document. To prevent wasting similar time and energy on your wedding, set up an organizational system. You don't have to spend money on a pricey wedding organizer. An ordinary three-ring binder with pockets and divider sections for organizing things by category will work just fine. On your computer set up a folder marked "wedding" and make sure all correspondence pertaining to the event goes in there for easy retrieval. Use the budget worksheet on page 202 to help you keep track of your expenditures, or an accounting software program can be a handy helper. (If you don't already have one, just put pencil to paper; learning a new program will just eat into your time.) The key is to find a system that works for you. Make one big checklist (and use the ones in this book) of everything that needs to get done, and cross off the tasks as you finish them.

Selecting Attendants

As soon as people know you're getting hitched and you've firmed up a date, the guessing game begins. Will your best buddies make it into the wedding party or only brothers and sisters? Will that cute little nephew get to walk down the aisle? Are you obligated to ask cousin Bob to be a groomsman because you were in his wedding a decade ago?

Who makes the cut and who doesn't is entirely up to you as a couple. Like whittling down a guest list, selecting attendants can be stressful. No one likes making someone feel left out or unimportant.

Though you don't have to rush into the decisions, it's a good idea to determine the attendants early on; it's only common courtesy to give an attendant plenty of notice (at least six months, if possible). Plus you'll have time to find a replacement if needed. (Don't rush into asking, though, until you know how many attendants the ceremony site can handle.) How do you finagle your way through this sensitive area? Consider these tips:

Pick a number. Decide how large or how small you want your wedding party. Having one person on each side to act as your witnesses is perfectly acceptable. Prefer zero? That's also doable, as long as you make arrangements for witnesses to sign the marriage certificate. If you want to supersize your wedding party, keep in mind that the costs will rise. You'll need to purchase more bouquets, boutonnieres, and attendant gifts. Depending upon who's paying for what, you may also end up with added costs for bridesmaids' dresses and tuxes. Think about the style of wedding you're having. Generally formal weddings have more attendants than informal ones. The ceremony site plays a big role too. Having six attendants swarming around a starry-eyed couple on a too-small altar may look more like a football-team huddle than a wedding party. Conversely, if you have a total of two attendants at a grand cathedral, guests may wonder if the rest of the wedding party suddenly took ill.

Set parameters. Perhaps you both only want immediate family members to stand up with you—voilà, you have an ironclad alibi that even your dearest friends will understand. Without getting too robotic, if you can establish some criteria, it's easier to rule in or rule out contenders for your wedding party. There's no obligation to ask a college roommate you haven't spoken to in two years to be in your wedding just because you talked about it during a 2 a.m. gab fest. Do you really want to look back on your wedding photos years from now and struggle to remember who that person is standing beside your brother? There's no rule that says you have to have equal numbers of this and that either. If you're the cool aunt and uncle that a gaggle of 12-and-under kids admires or you're blending families, put them all in the wedding and parade them down the aisle as a group.

Do you want kids? Hold on—we're not talking about the pitter-patter of little feet. We're talking about flower girls and ring bearers. It's a rare bride and groom who doesn't have a cute-as-a-button niece, nephew, cousin, or neighbor that some adult is eager to dole out. Determine if adding a youngster into the mix is something you want to do or something you want to steer clear of at all costs. Remember: Kids say and do the darnedest things when you least want them to. But if you have young children or there are stepchildren involved, this may be a great way to make them feel like part of the family. Preteen and teen children are typically referred to as "junior" attendants; flower girls and ring bearers are typically under 10 years old.

Personalize it. Let's face it: Not everyone enjoys being in a wedding. Some people hate—even fear—donning a dress or tux and being a center of attention. Others might not have the money to spend on showering you with gifts and paying for the proper attire. Or they might not have the bucks or vacation time to flit off to the exotic locale you've chosen. And your pregnant sister may not find the thought of waddling down an aisle appealing. As you discuss possible attendants as a couple, factor in each individual's situation, likes, and dislikes. Certain "positions," so to speak, also carry a certain responsibility with them, so make sure those are also suited to the individual. (See "Who Does What?," page 49, for more information.) Jot down the names of people you're both considering and talk things over. In case you're wondering, a bride can have a male attendant, and a groom can have a female one. To avoid complications, refer to members of your wedding party as "attendants" rather than bridesmaids or groomsmen.

When you ask someone if he or she will be an attendant, the soft-sell approach is always best. Most people are too courteous to say no—even if deep down they want to—so tell them to take a bit of time to think about it and that you understand if they say no. Be sure to clarify what's expected of them, such as whether they will have to pay for the attire (and an estimate on how much that will be) and exactly when they would need to be available (for example, can the person skip the rehearsal if need be?). In the long run, it's better to have someone say no than resent saying yes.

Finding Help

Remember back at the beginning of this chapter when we said you were the CEO of your wedding? We weren't kidding; you really do need to approach your wedding the same way the CEO of a company would approach a big project. As top dog, you also get to delegate.

If you're lucky enough to be CEO of a billion-dollar enterprise, you can delegate in style by hiring a wedding planner without so much as batting an eye or looking at the budget to see if it's doable. If you're a fledgling upstart, delegating might mean forming committees of relatives, friends, and neighbors.

Chances are you've already received some phone calls or e-mails from eager beavers willing to help you out with this or with that. If not, you might have some names swirling in your mind. (If you don't, refer back to "Timeline Checklist" on page 38, which outlines everything that you have to get done; this reality check will help you realize you can't do it alone, or even just the two of you.) Take volunteers up on their offer, and solicit helpers. Some tasks naturally fall on certain members of the wedding party (see "Who Does What?" **opposite**), but you'll need to clarify if that person is really willing to do them.

Expert Advice **The wedding day is nerve-racking enough without having to worry about decorating the venues or making sure the food gets out on the buffet table. As such, plan to have a wedding coordinator or trusty friend or relative be the go-to person. "The more you overextend yourself, the less fun you'll have," wedding planner Matt O'Dorisio says.**

Delegating doesn't mean handing over the reigns and losing control (well, unless you have complete trust that the person doing the task will perform it to your satisfaction). As with all good bosses, choose trustworthy, responsible people to help you out with tasks. Match their responsibilities with their skills and personalities. You don't want people who crack under pressure acting as the host or hostess (and unofficial ambassadors) of your reception. If a good friend is a great seamstress, but is notoriously late getting things done, he or she may not be the best choice for stitching up a gown on two weeks' notice.

Your "committees" can be as formal or as informal as you like. The important thing is to find out who's willing and who's able to do what, and write down the assignments and time frame for completion. There are some tasks that traditionally fall on certain family members or attendants.

Who Does What?

Tradition dictates that certain attendants and family members have certain obligations: You know, the bride's parents write out the check for the wedding, the best man throws a wild bachelor party, and the ushers slather the newlyweds' getaway vehicle with shaving cream—or not! Traditional guidelines and roles don't fit everyone's situation or even their idea of fun. With blended families, divorced parents, and second marriages, the situation can be even trickier. For instance, should the stepfather who raised the bride or the biological father escort the bride? More on those potentially sticky situations in "And What Do You Do?" on page 53.

Short of handing out a decree on who shall do what, what can you do? The best approach is to make it clear—in a nice, polite kind of way. When you ask people to be part of your wedding, be up front about what that entails. Then they can decide whether they're up for the job. A little lightening up may be in order too. No matter how well you hide your car, there's a good chance a sleuthing usher is going to find it.

Let the following traditions be a guide for helping determine which friends or relatives are most suited for each job and what you can expect. The most important thing is to make sure you clarify expectations with the specific individuals, so everyone is on the same page.

Maid/Matron of honor. This person acts as the bride's right-hand person before, during, and after the wedding. As such, choose your maid (single woman) of honor, matron (married woman) of honor, or honor attendant (male friend or relative) carefully. Someone may be your close sister or best friend, but if she's prone to being disorganized, tardy, or irresponsible, be prepared to take on extra tasks and have a few more headaches. These are specific tasks that traditionally fall on this person:

- Helps with prewedding tasks, including shopping for dresses.
- Acts as committee chair for bridal/couples shower.
- Holds bride's bouquet and adjusts train when needed during ceremony.
- Holds groom's ring during ceremony.
- Signs the marriage license as a witness.
- Gives a toast at reception.
- Makes sure bride's personal belongings that were brought to the ceremony are taken to the designated location after the wedding and/or reception.
- Ensures that gifts (and bridal gown, if instructed) are transported to the designated location after the reception, often with the help of other attendants.
- Calms the bride throughout everything.

Best man. This is the go-to guy (or in some cases gal) for the groom. Yes, the best man is indeed the one to organize a bachelor party—and hopefully the person is sensitive enough to know what type of party both the bride and groom would approve of, or if the groom even wants a party. In addition to the bachelor party, here are other best man responsibilities:

- Occupies groom the hours leading up to the wedding.
- Gets groom to the ceremony.
- Holds bride's ring during ceremony.
- Signs the marriage license as a witness.
- At couple's request (and with their money) makes sure payments and honorariums are given to the officiant, musicians, servers, and other appropriate people.
- Gives a toast at reception.
- Returns any rental attire on behalf of the groom and wedding party.
- Ensures that gifts are transported to the designated location after the reception, often with help of other attendants.

Bridesmaids. Here's a little secret about getting the most out of your bridesmaids: Don't dress them in something you wouldn't be caught in. If you do, they'll be busy finding the nearest coatrack to hide behind rather than lending a helping hand. Aside from showing up, the biggest task that falls on bridesmaids is to assist the maid/matron of honor or honor attendant with planning and running the bridal/couples shower. Bridesmaids also can be tapped to help with prewedding tasks, such as shopping for dresses. On the wedding day you can also have bridesmaids hand out balloons, bubbles, bells, or other items guests will use as the newlyweds leave the ceremony site.

Groomsmen. Like the best man, the groomsmen can help keep the groom occupied and calm in the hours leading up to the ceremony. They also can assist the best man with rounding up and returning any rental attire.

Flower girl and ring bearer. The biggest role this mini bride and groom have is to look cute. The phrase "ring bearer" is somewhat of a misnomer; most couples don't entrust a little guy to care for the rings. Instead the ring bearer's loot is usually nothing more than fake rings, if any at all. A flower girl traditionally drops flower petals—real or artificial—down the aisle or carries a basket of flowers before the bride enters. She's traditionally preceded by the ring bearer, though sometimes the two walk side-by-side.

Ushers. Everyone knows that ushers escort guests to their seats, but a good usher does more than that. He or she makes sure all those little details are in place: matches out so candles can be lit, reserved signs in place on seats, taking care of an aisle runner if one is being used. Ushers can also be in charge of making sure the cards and gifts are taken to a designated location at the end of the day. And, oh yes, ushers usually take it upon themselves to decorate the bride and groom's vehicle, often in cahoots with the groomsmen. As a general rule, plan on one usher per 50 guests.

Bride's parents. Traditionally the bride's parents foot the bill for the shindig, minus the rehearsal dinner and perhaps the liquor at the reception. As discussed earlier, those traditions have changed greatly, and often the couple pays for all or a big portion of the wedding and reception. The bride's father traditionally escorts the bride down the aisle; sometimes, both parents do. If the father is deceased, the mother, a brother, an uncle, or any close friend can step in. If there's a father and a stepfather in the picture, it's the bride's call as to whom she wants to do the honor; unless the bride and biological father are estranged, it's usually the biological father who escorts his daughter. Depending on the relationships, the bride could even choose to have both men walk her down the aisle—an unconventional touch, but a way to show the family is united. The father also has the first dance with the bride, after the newlyweds have had their dance together. The mother is typically the bride's trusty advisor throughout the planning.

Groom's parents. Consider them among the lucky—at least if you follow traditional guidelines. Their responsibilities traditionally include paying for the rehearsal dinner and, perhaps, the liquor at the reception as well as a wedding album with photos they've selected. Some groom's parents would be happy to be more involved, so find out where yours stand on the issue.

Bride's personal attendant. As trips to the beauty salon have become commonplace—or bringing hair stylists and makeup artists to the ceremony site—the role of a personal attendant has diminished. Still a personal attendant can be a handy helper to pin corsages on people, fetch a bottle of nail polish, or do a quick pressing job on a wrinkled slip.

Reception hosts. Consider these people your goodwill ambassadors. Because they'll be greeting guests at the reception, a big smile and an outgoing personality are prerequisites for the job. Typically there's one host (or couple) from the bride's side and one from the groom's side. The reason for this is to help ensure that most guests will see a familiar face, or at least have a connection that can spark a conversation. Of course choosing relatives isn't necessary because the hosts' primary job is to steer guests inside to a coat check, guest book, or champagne station.

Guest-book attendant. You can choose an adult to tend to the guest book, but it's a job that's perfectly suited to a preteen or teen who may feel especially honored you asked. You may want to designate an adult to make sure the book, pen, and accompanying materials get transported from the ceremony site to the reception site.

Servers. You can tap a wide range of family or friends to pour punch, cut cake, or serve food. Tending bar requires a bit more skill if you're serving mixed drinks. Tread lightly if you're asking adults to do these types of jobs; some people may consider it menial labor and would rather be sitting at a table mingling with other guests.

Honorary guests. If there's someone who's special to you, but you can't figure out an official job for him or her, designate that person as an honorary guest. A grandparent, the family you lived with during an exchange program abroad, or simply a longtime family friend are worthy candidates. Mention them in the wedding program, give them a corsage or boutonniere, and have an usher escort them to their seats just before the processional.

And What Do You Do?

Now that you know who does what, you may be wondering what you do if ... your parents are divorced, you have children, or you want to invite an ex. Today's families come in many forms. Consider these guidelines to tone down any possible melodrama.

Divorced parents. This is usually more of an issue if it's the bride's parents who are divorced because the bride's side is usually more involved in the planning. If a stepfather raised the bride rather than the biological father, it also raises the question of who escorts the bride down the aisle. The answer is that it's up to the bride; she knows whom she's closest to and who's the father figure, regardless of DNA. You'll have to tread lightly if there are divorced parents in the picture—especially if they're not on speaking terms. Whether the divorce is on the bride's side, groom's side, or both, talk to each parent individually. You'll need to find out what role they expect to have in your wedding (including financial support), and you need to express what you expect from them (including no bad behavior on your wedding day or, really, during the entire process). Your wedding may conjure up memories of their own wedding, so keeping emotions in check may be difficult for them. As such, be mindful of keeping each parent in the loop about your plans, and, depending on the relations, make sure they have some distance at showers, the wedding ceremony, and the reception. Seat them at separate tables, separate chairs, separate pews.

Stepparents, stepsisters, and stepbrothers. The same rules apply for the "step category" as they do for divorced parents. You'll have to tread lightly to keep family feuds at bay. Think through the seating at the wedding and reception so your mother doesn't end up next to your stepmother, or so your father doesn't end up between both—it would likely be awkward for all of them.

Your children. Whether you're blending families or just one of you has a child, find a special role for the child or children. Some couples include a child as part of the vows; for instance, the groom pledges his love and commitment to both the bride and her child, who's also standing at the altar. A preteen or teen can serve as a junior attendant, or a group of kids can form a choir to sing a special song. Hopefully you've talked through any adoption or legal issues by now; if not, put down this book and do that.

Former spouses, boyfriends, or girlfriends. There's no reason for either of you to invite an ex to anything—no matter how much you want to stick it to them and show them what a catch you have. Exceptions might include if an ex happens to be a mutual friend or if a former spouse is there to tend to your young child (a grandparent or sibling, though, might be a better option).

Don't Forget ...

There's a good reason why you may find there's not enough hours in the day. How can you find the perfect reception site when everyone is asking you when you're available for a shower or when you're going to to officially announce your engagement in the first place? Before you move on to the big details, try to get three things crossed off your list—or at least penciled onto your calendar: the engagement announcement, registering for gifts, and showers/parties.

Engagement Announcement

Extra! Extra! If you want to let the world—or at least some locals—know about your pending nuptials, spread the word via a newspaper announcement. More often than not, these announcements are fodder for scrapbooks. If you're not in to sentimental stuff like that or you don't care to have everyone in town clued in to your plans, you'll save a few bucks by skipping the announcement.

In recent years many newspapers have started charging a nominal fee for placing an announcement. Call the newspaper (or newspapers, if your spouse-to-be or immediate families live in another city) to find out its policy. Some will have forms you'll need to complete and sign and require a daytime phone number so an editor can verify the information (one can never be too cautious about prank engagements, after all!). Others, usually smaller weeklies, won't mind if you just drop in and scribble out the details.

Speaking of which, details typically included in the announcement are the bride's and groom's names, occupations, and often when and where they attended and graduated from high school and/or college. Parents' names are usually listed, along with the wedding date. Announcements are published anywhere from a year before the wedding to just before it; find out if the newspaper has a policy on the time frame. While you're on the phone, find out what the policy is for submitting a write-up and photo after the wedding; ask the editor to send any forms for that along with the engagement announcement.

A photo of the couple typically accompanies the announcement, but sometimes only the bride's photo appears. You don't have to have an official engagement photo, unless it's on your priorities list and factored into your budget. To save money, scour already published engagement photos to find poses you like, then have a friend or relative snap a roll of film. If you don't know anyone who's handy with a camera, find out what a photo studio at a department store charges. You may have to endure a few crying kids and parents trying too hard to get them to smile pretty for the camera, but you can usually get a few pictures for a decent price. Other options are photography teachers or students at a local high school or college.

Alternatives to a traditional newspaper announcement include sending an e-mail message (a tad impersonal, but a time- and cost-saver—and also a great time to ask for updated mailing addresses for the guest list); sending a save the date card (more on that in Chapter 3, page 86); hosting an informal party to make the announcement to your inner circle; or hiring a skywriter to spell it out from above (bet you haven't budgeted for that one, have you?).

Registering for Gifts

Ten toasters, seven blenders, four slow cookers … oh joy! There's no reason you have to feign excitement about receiving a gift you don't want, don't need, or already have. Though you don't have a license to be ungrateful, you can be proactive to ward off unwanted gifts. It's called the gift registry.

Take a few hours early on to figure out where you want to register and call the stores to find out their policies. Do they allow exchanges and returns? Must you have a gift receipt? Sign up early (assuming the store doesn't have time frame restrictions) so you have one less thing on your to-do list later on.

To simplify things for everyone, limit your gift registry to one or two stores, preferably ones that are widely accessible in your area or across the country, if you have a lot of faraway guests. You may want to choose one upscale department store if you're registering for china and crystal, and one discount store or home center for practical stuff like, well, a toaster, blender, and slow cooker. But, come on, you can do better. How about camping equipment for your wilderness honeymoon, a lawnmower for your new home, or a new set of dumbbells for your vow to get fit together? More and more couples are putting less traditional items on their wish lists—especially couples who are older or who have already been married and have the basics.

Registering online has made the whole gift registry thing easier than ever, and it's a gesture cyberspace-crazed guests will appreciate. They can shop 24 hours a day without leaving home, and gifts can be shipped right to your door. (Translation: Guests don't have to drag a package along to the wedding, and you don't have to drag it home.) Depending on the company, gifts may be held and shipped at one time, streamlining things even more. As with everything, make sure you're dealing with a reputable company and that you know the details of its registry policy, including returns and exchanges. The downside of an online registry is that the recipient usually ends up paying postage if the item is returned, but if the online site has a store in your area, you usually can swap things there.

Though most guests will be happy that you've registered somewhere and offered ideas on what you can use, some will do their own thing. Variety is the spice of life, so, whether you need the gift or not, smile and say thanks. If you can't return the gift to the store and you really don't want it, there's a good chance a charity will—even if that charity is your just-out-of-college brother.

One final thing about gifts: Don't request that guests give you money instead of tangible items—unless someone has specifically asked what you want. In a worst-case scenario, return unwanted gifts to the store (assuming you know where they came from), take the money, and thank the giver for the original gift.

Showers and Parties

Not only are you the CEO of your wedding, you're also the COA—as in center of attention. More than likely, one or both of you will be feted at showers, engagement parties, and, later, bachelor and bachelorette parties. Traditionally the maid/matron of honor or honor attendant hosts the bridal shower. Friends, family, and coworkers may also want to throw their own bashes.

If you think one, and only one, shower or party is enough, speak up. If you think no shower or party is needed, speak up on that too. It's a rare guest who will be disappointed if they don't get to play a silly game or purchase yet another gift. Letting your wishes be known early on will also alleviate awkward situations—say when a close friend decides he or she wants to host a party in your honor, thereby stepping on the toes of your honor attendant who is already planning something for the same day.

Quick Tip Feeling charitable? Have guests make a donation to the charity of your choice in lieu of giving you a gift. This simplifies things on your end (no registering for gifts, no packages overtaking a room), and you'll have the satisfaction of doing a good deed. Designating a charitable donation is a growing trend, especially with couples who already have what they need or those who have been previously married.

Dos and Don'ts

Hang on! The next few weeks, months, or year will be a roller coaster. When you feel like you're in over your head, refer back to this list.

Do

- Make a list of priorities and stick to it. To keep focused on what's truly important, put "Marrying the person I love" at the top of the list. If the caterer backs out or the dresses arrive in the wrong color, look at your No. 1 priority.

- Take family and friends up on their offers to help. Look in a mirror and repeat this sentence: I can't do it all.

- Be flexible. You'll get better deals, have more options, and may be able to get something that would otherwise be out of your reach. Your top reception site that's booked on a Saturday—the most popular day for weddings—may be available Friday evening or on Sunday morning and at a discount. (Sunday weddings have become popular, so discounted prices are getting rarer.)

- Make time for each other. Set a weekly date night for just the two of you and try to talk about anything but the wedding plans.

- Stick to your normal routine as much as possible. Exercise, eat properly, and get plenty of sleep.

Don't

- Let others sway you. When you cut through all the wispy veils and appetizer samples, this day is about you. It's not the wedding that your parents, your in-laws-to-be, or your best friend never had. The day belongs to you and your future spouse, so make it what you both want it to be—not what someone else thinks it should be.

- Get carried away. Your budget will suffer, and you'll feel too guilty to enjoy all those little extras you splurged on.

- Expect perfection. There will be hiccups. There will be stresses. Get used to it—and laugh it off.

- Forget to update the budget. If you don't continually replace the estimated costs with the actual expenses, you may wind up in the hole.

- Forget to say thank you. These are two words attendants who go the extra mile to help you find attire, the people who host showers, the parents who chip in their hard-earned money, and the guests who show their support won't tire of hearing.

Couples showers are gaining popularity, so you may want to offer that as an alternative to a bride-only gathering, or even as a replacement for the bachelor and bachelorette parties. A great thing about a couples shower is that it gets both the groom—who is often left out of prewedding parties—and the bride involved. Additionally, a couples shower provides a chance for some guests who may not have yet met the groom (or bride, as the case may be) to get to know the person before an initial encounter at the wedding.

Friends may want to throw the shower anywhere from six months to three weeks before the wedding. If you're going to have one, consider doing it early. If you wait until you're thick into the planning, you may be too stressed to really enjoy the gathering or to appreciate all the work that went into feting you.

A party you may not be expecting is an engagement party. Formal engagement parties have become passé for many couples, though your close friends may insist that you gather for a backyard barbecue or dinner at a favorite hangout. Take them up on the offer as a way to celebrate with your inner circle of friends before things get too crazy and you're consumed with wedding plans. Just make it known that you want to keep things simple and casual so you don't burden anyone with more costs on decorations or gifts.

Expert Advice Don't get so carried away with all the wedding stuff that you forget to showcase your best assets: the bride and groom. "Weddings are weddings—there's food, there's dancing, there's flowers," wedding planner Sally Steele says. "But what you really want to show off is the couple and who they are."

Creative

Put your personal stamp on the

License

big day with themes and beyond.

chapter
2

The church, the white dress, the banquet hall, the tiered cake topped with a plastic bride and groom. If those iconic wedding-day images don't flip your switch, then sit back and read on. With a little imagination—well, maybe a lot of imagination—you can have a one-of-a-kind gala that reflects your personalities, interests, and comfort level. How, you ask?

For starters, toss the rulebook filled with preconceived notions of what a wedding looks and feels like. "If you throw away rules A, B, and C, then you're forced to think 'What do I want? What represents us?'" wedding planner Jackson Lowell says. "It's all about figuring out what you like and where you come from. Don't give me the typical A, B, and C. Give me YOUR A, B, and C."

Say, for example, you love sailing. How about dropping anchor at a marina or exchanging vows on a yacht? No way, says your budget? Skip the yacht for a pontoon or a houseboat you can rent by the day or hour. Or move the soiree to the beach at a small lake, a riverboat, a backyard pond, or a water park where you won't feel landlocked.

The only rule should be that no one has to be married to the traditional image of "wedding." Many couples—and society in general—put themselves in the proverbial box and don't dare think outside it. "Outside of that box, what would you do?" Jackson urges couples to think. Ask yourself this question at every turn as you plan your big day, and you'll open yourself up to fun and creative alternatives to the expected. If you play it right, your unconventional choices may ultimately save you money.

Theme Weddings

I f you mention to people that you're having a theme wedding, the reactions may range from a puzzled "What's that?" to jaw-dropping horror. For some people a theme wedding translates into something crazy-wild, such as the bride and groom dressing as Tarzan and Jane and swinging from branches on their way to the altar.

A theme wedding can be as crazy, kitschy, or as sophisticated as you want to make it. You can scream theme by donning costumes, beating your chest, and getting married in a makeshift jungle if that's the beat you march to. You can sashay down the checkerboard floor of a '50s diner in a poodle skirt and rolled-up jeans. Or you can let the theme reveal itself in more subtle ways, such as by choosing a favorite color for a "true blue" wedding. Whatever spin you put on it, the beauty of a theme wedding is that it gives you focus. You know, for example, whether to shop for all-things blue or whether to shop for loincloths—or whatever the theme at hand is.

Another plus is that a theme wedding can make far-flung fantasies a reality. If you can't afford the Parisian wedding of your dreams, for example, turn your reception into your French fantasy. Create a homemade scaled-down replica of the Eiffel Tower and transform the dining area into a sidewalk cafe with street musicians and pastries—similar to what wedding planner Alan Dunn did for one lucky couple featured on **For Better or For Worse**. Hold the event by a scenic river, and you can bring the Seine to you.

Intrigued? Consider these themes and approaches—some heavy on theme, and others just mildly different. Even if you don't want to take things to the extreme, you can glean ideas that can be tweaked to be more suitable for your own rendition. Check out the photo-filled section, starting on page 209, to see a wide variety of themes the **For Better or For Worse** wedding planners have brought to life. Though a theme wedding almost commands decoration, it doesn't mean you have to spend wildly. Get creative with the venue you choose and use your imagination on decorations (red-chili-pepper lights snagged at an end-of-summer sale can spice up a "south of the border" soiree) so your pocketbook doesn't take a hit. Consider these ideas:

School days. So you fell in love in the hallowed halls of high school? Rent out the school for a high-school sweetheart shindig. The front steps or the auditorium stage is your altar, the cafeteria is your dining hall, and the gym is your dance floor. Maybe you were a bit older when you became starry-eyed. College campuses can be great wedding settings; most have an icon, such as a fountain, campanile, or brick archway, that can make a beautiful backdrop for an outdoor affair. To keep from getting in the way of backpack-clad students or a protest on central campus, schedule the event when students are on break. Of course you'll need permission from school officials to use the premises.

Fairy-tale ending. Even if you take the prince and princess out of the church, you can have a wedding fit for royalty. Give yourself a fairy-tale wedding by booking the nearest castle. If there's no such thing in your area, find a grand historic venue or house, ideally in a secluded setting. For a Cinderella-style wedding—such as one wedding planner Angie Bloom Hewett planned for a couple featured on **For Better or For Worse**—bring in the trumpeters and roll out an aisle runner with the phrase "And they lived happily every after" on it. Use special florist's paint to tip white roses with 24-karat gold (see page 242 for instructions).

Groovy, baby. Relive the '60s and treat guests to a swinging good time, just like wedding planner Matt O'Dorisio did for one hip couple. Make invitations from a spin-art machine designed for children, then set it up at the reception to give guests of all ages something to do. Lava-style lamps can become centerpieces (see page 234 for instructions).

Seasonal splendor. Planning a wedding around the season in which it takes place is an easy way to have a theme wedding without anyone rolling his or her eyes and thinking you've lost your mind. An autumn wedding gets into the spirit with gourds, pumpkins, potted mums, and bales of hay as decorations. Warm apple cider takes the place of punch, and frosted pumpkin bars can stand in for traditional white or chocolate cake for a harvest hoedown. Hold the event at an apple orchard, barn, or park to capture the seasonal color as a backdrop. For a winter wedding, create a wonderland with white faux-fur draping tables, an ice sculpture, and white Christmas lights. If there's an ice rink out back, all the better. Money permitting, light up the sky with an all-white fireworks display. Holidays also offer easy theme opportunities. Think holly and ivy at Christmas or stars and stripes around the Fourth of July. A word of warning about getting hitched around holidays: You'll pay more for flowers and often the venues.

Got game? Usually it's the bride who has all the fantasies swirling in her mind. A sports-theme wedding, though, may be a dream come true for the groom (or a sports-minded couple). If your wildest dream is to tie the knot on the pitcher's mound of your favorite pro team, ask if it's doable; there's always the high school stadium if it doesn't pan out. Reception food is easy: Popcorn, hot dogs, and beer served in a skybox or a reception hall after the first pitch is thrown. Other game ideas: Transform the reception site into a casino, or get out the croquet sets for an English-style outdoor setting.

Time travel. If there's a locale or era you're fond of, let it launch the theme of your special day. Evoke the image of 1950s Havana with cigar boxes filled with roses and tropical flowers for centerpieces and wedding programs that are rolled up to look like cigars and displayed in cigar boxes. Wedding planner Jackson Lowell did just that for a one-of-a-kind celebration. Or bring out the flavor of old Madrid by setting the event in a Spanish mission-style park with plenty of red accents and a flamenco band.

An affair to remember. A rooftop setting has a certain air about it. Think Cary Grant in **An Affair to Remember**. If the top of the Empire State Building is off limits, rent a terrace or rooftop from a corporation, a high-rise condo, or hotel—just like Angie Bloom Hewett did for one memorable ceremony. The soaring-above-the-fray setting alone is theme enough.

Getting it in black and white. In a world of color, why not black and white? It's classy and elegant and conjures images of screen legends and their romances. From an attire standpoint, you can score points by dressing bridesmaids in simple black dresses—they're the rare attendant dresses that have

Quick Tip Beware when considering a nontraditional venue for your wedding or reception. A beach or a private estate may seem enticing, but it may demand extra work (and extra money) from you. "With some of these places, couples don't realize everything that goes with it," says wedding planner Matt O'Dorisio. "You just don't realize that you need to bring in every napkin, every fork, every teaspoon, every salt and pepper shaker." The bottom line? Know exactly what you're getting—and what you're not getting—before you commit to any venue.

a fighting chance of being worn again to a cocktail party or black-tie affair. Other color combos can be equally sophisticated. A silver and white theme, for example, lends sparkle and elegance.

Global Traditions

A theme wedding isn't the only way to personalize your day. By celebrating your heritage or ethnicity, you can expose guests to customs they may not be familiar with, making the day something fun and new for them. An African-American couple may choose to jump the broom, or male guests will discover they must pin money to a Cuban bride's dress in exchange for a dance.

The degree to which you follow the customs is up to you, though you'll need to make sure key players are in the loop about your wishes and plans. If you don't want a formal homage, you can have fun incorporating aspects of your heritage in more lighthearted ways, such as serving a canolli cake at an Italian reception. You can bring in the customs from your two different backgrounds, and you can incorporate elements that have no connection to you but you find endearing.

When planning a ceremony that will pay homage to your background—even in part—be sure to check with the officiant on any restrictions, as well as for guidance on what is commonly done. You'll also need to study up on the traditions; a parent or grandparent can be a great source. Here's a look at some ethnic traditions:

African. The traditions vary greatly depending on the country. "Jumping the broom" is a tradition incorporated into some weddings as a symbol of leaping over the threshold into married life. The tradition dates back to slavery, when slaves who were not allowed to legally marry leaped over a broom.

American Indian. Color plays prominently in the ceremony. The bride's dress features colors that symbolize the earth's four corners: black for north, blue for south, white for east, and yellow for west. White (for male) and yellow (for female) corn is formed into mush to symbolize the bonding between the groom and bride; the couple shares the mush.

Chinese. Red and gold—symbols of happiness and wealth—play prominently in Chinese customs, starting with guests receiving invitations wrapped in red paper. During the ceremony, the couple shows their respect to their parents and other elders; the bride offers tea to the groom's family (each family member sips the tea), and the groom gives an offering to the bride's side. To ward off evil spirits, firecrackers are lit after the ceremony.

Czech. A notable custom in a Czech wedding is bridesmaids pinning rosemary sprigs on guests as a symbol of fertility.

Dutch. After the ceremony the couple plants lily-of-the-valley in their garden. When the flowers bloom each year, it's a signal for the couple to renew their love.

English. Traditionally a young girl scatters flower petals as the bride makes her way to the ceremony site—the goal being to pave a joyous path for the bride's life. The bride sometimes carries a horseshoe as a sign of good luck. Fruitcake is the traditional wedding dessert.

French. Laurel leaves take the place of rice or birdseed to toss as the couple leaves the ceremony site.

German. After a civil ceremony for a small group of friends and relatives and a party where plates are broken as a sign of good luck, the couple has a religious ceremony, followed by a reception. The celebration is typically a three-day affair.

Greek. During the ceremony, the bride and groom are literally dubbed queen and king for the day (the best man crowns them king and queen). The "Circle Dance," during which guests hold hands and move in rhythm, is traditionally done at the reception.

Indian. The bride's hands and feet are painted with henna patterns before the ceremony. After the ceremony, flower petals are tossed, usually by the groom's brothers, to ward off evil spirits.

Irish. The Claddagh band may be the most commonly recognized Irish symbol. The ring, often an engagement ring, features two hands holding a heart with a crown; it was first made by an Irishman who had been taken prisoner and unable to return immediately to his love. During the ceremony, the ring is placed on the bride's finger so the hands and crown face in (only married people are to wear it in that position). At the reception, the groom is hoisted in a chair and presented to the guests in a custom called the "janting char."

Italian. Before a hearty and boisterous reception, Italian newlyweds historically greeted villagers and had to saw through a log to symbolize that they must work together. (Reenacting this tradition at your modern-day reception is sure to catch guests' attention!) Candy-covered almonds typically given to guests at the reception represent the bitter and the sweet parts of life.

Japanese. During the wedding ceremony, the bride and groom share sake from three cups as a symbol of happiness, luck, and of solemnizing the marriage. Parents join in at the end to symbolize the unity of the two families.

Jewish. Many people are familiar with at least a few Jewish traditions: the groom breaking a napkin-covered wineglass with his foot, guests shouting "Mazel Tov," and, at the reception, guests dancing the celebratory Hora. Less familiar traditions include the bride and groom standing under a canopy called a chuppah during the ceremony and, at the reception, distributing pieces of challah, a braided egg bread, to each guest as a sign of good luck. The wedding ceremony is usually held on a Saturday after sundown or on a Sunday. (For instructions on making a chuppah, designed by wedding planner Sally Steele, see page 228.)

Korean. In addition to wearing a colorful silk gown with white sleeves, a bride applies a red dot to each cheek to ward off evil spirits. During the ceremony the groom introduces his parents to the bride. The groom's father lobs red dates at the bride as a signal he wants many grandchildren.

Latin American. The flower girl and ring bearer are decked out as miniature versions of the bride and groom.

Mexican. The groom presents 13 gold coins to the bride as his promise to support her. A small chest of coins, called an arras, symbolizing wealth and strength, is blessed during the ceremony.

Moravian. Anyone who has attended a Moravian celebration at Christmas will find similar elements at a wedding, with handmade beeswax candles casting a golden glow. The couple lights a candle, and then lights the candle of a guest, who in turn lights the candle of the next guest.

Polish. The couple's parents greet the newlyweds at the reception to bestow bread and salt, which represent the prosperity and bitterness they may face.

Russian. At the reception, champagne glasses are thrown to the floor after the couple has been toasted. The broken glass is a sign of happiness ahead. The couple's car (or other getaway vehicle) also shows their preference for their firstborn. If they want a girl, they tie a doll to the front. If they want a boy, it's a toy bear.

Scandinavian. Birch branches decorate the church and altar. To keep the couple away from evil, pieces of fabric called care cloths hide them during the final blessings.

Scottish. The groom dons a kilt representative of his "clan." A bagpiper provides music, though often it's reserved for the recessional only.

Destination Weddings

Destination weddings have surged in popularity. The couple and guests whisk themselves to the chosen location—a lodge in the Canadian wilderness, a sugary beach in the Caribbean, an estate two states away, or a Vegas chapel filled with Elvis look-alikes.

There's good news and bad news with destination weddings, and, depending on your priorities, the good news could be the bad news and vice versa. For example, a destination wedding forces you to whittle the guest list. Hurrah for those of you wanting a small wedding; not ideal if you were planning on filling guests to the rafters. Other pluses (or minuses): A destination wedding is like a vacation for you and your closest friends and relatives (which means you might have to put up with them for four days straight, when you'd rather be swooning by yourselves). It takes a lot of coordination to pull off a faraway celebration (which means a local wedding planner or other local authority is almost a must, unless you're opting for a package wedding deal at a theme park or other place known for its weddings).

The biggest drawback of a destination wedding is cost. Things don't come cheap, so if you're on a budget, you'll really need to pare down the amenities and the number of guests. Angie Bloom Hewett recalls tropical weddings where every little detail—chandeliers, silverware, even the service crews—had to be flown in, and extra security was hired to guard the tent. Legal matters can be tricky too. Some countries may require two officiants; others require a trip to an attorney's office once you get there. "You have to find out exactly what the laws are," she says. "It's very different from country to country; it's all over the map." Another consideration: Make sure you get a certified copy of the marriage certificate; you'll need this whenever you need to show proof that you're married. When you get married out of the country, you don't have the luxury of a quick run or call to the nearby courthouse to have them dig up the record, so keep the certified copy in a safe place. One more consideration: The weather and time of year. If you are dreaming of a tropical locale, keep the season in mind—while rates may be lower during hurricane and tropical storm season, it may not be a risk worth taking.

If your mind is set on a destination wedding but not on whittling the guest list to just you and your two best buddies, it's time to get even more creative. Five days of fun in Hawaii, complete with a welcome-night luau, may be out of the picture, but a weekend getaway to a place 50 miles away may be a welcome reprieve from the ordinary. The more off-the-beaten-path the venue, the more likely you can afford it and the more likely it's available. Some ideas to consider include the following:

Wine and dine. An outdoor wedding among grapevines and open skies can be a breath of fresh air. Check local wineries to see if they fling open their doors to brides and grooms. Most wineries offer tastings (fun for guests) and many have dining facilities.

Bed-and-breakfast. Don't let the size of the house fool you: Many bed-and-breakfasts have expansive and pretty grounds and do the bulk of their business catering to large groups. Find out if the bed-and-breakfast operator is willing to prepare reception food or will allow you to have it catered in. A B&B set out in the country may have the ambiance of an English estate and feel like a grand getaway without the airfare.

Getting there is half the fun. One of Jackson Lowell's fond memories is when guests boarded a trolley to and from the ceremony site, passing through historical neighborhoods on the way. The trolley ride was entertainment in and of itself. A horse-drawn wagon is a similar option (farmers, state fairs, and festival organizers are good places to start to find such transportation). A dinner train can give guests the feeling of an adventure, even though they're just going a few miles down the track and back.

Quick Tip Don't be fooled by the pictures you see on the Internet or in brochures. If you're planning a destination wedding, visit the area first, says wedding planner Erika Shay. "A lot of the places look completely different when you visit them in person—they can look smaller than you'd ever imagine," she says. As such it's best to make a quick trip to the locale, and while you're there, you can find a local wedding planner or hotel official you trust to complete the details.

Other Ideas

Short of jumping out of an airplane, what else can you do to ensure your wedding isn't more of the same ol', same ol'? Here are some out-of-the-box ideas to consider:

Surprise! We're getting married! Celebrities have done it, so why not you? If you like spontaneity or crave an easygoing atmosphere, invite friends and family over for a party. Little do they know, this party is actually your wedding. Keeping things on the down-low eliminates the stress of meddlesome parents and the headache of trying to please everyone. So what if your guests are wearing shorts and jeans, while the bride and groom are dressed to the nines? Just remember, while you may enjoy the surprise, some family members who have more traditional views of what a wedding should be may not—having hoped for more warning time.

Weekday celebration. Want a really good deal on a venue—and probably even your number-one choice? Hold your wedding during the week. Granted, this may not be ideal for guests, especially out-of-towners. But if you want a small gathering, a weeknight wedding is a good way to keep things, including the expenses, short and sweet. Vendors often charge much less on a weekday than on weekends.

Love connection. If you're striking out on unique places and creative ways to personalize your day, think back to your engagement. If the question was popped at the county fair, get married there and treat guests to cotton candy and a ride on a Ferris wheel. If you get lucky, you might be able to rent out the grounds a few hours before the fair officially opens to the public. If the fair is over, rent one of the buildings and bring in your own cotton-candy machine and set up carnival-style game booths. If you were communing with nature when you got engaged, pitch some tents in the woods and turn your wedding into a two-day retreat with guests huddled around a campfire. A ceremony or reception set where you met, first declared your love for one another, or got engaged is a natural setting to begin the next chapter of your life.

Don't Forget ...

If your adventurous side is still aching to be released after you've read this chapter, take a deep breath before you start plotting out the daring details. The following considerations, which we touched on previously, need your undivided attention before you get locked into something you'll end up regretting:

Money, honey. Make sure your budget can truly handle a one-of-a-kind wedding. Do you really have any clue how much it costs to rent a sky-diving plane and instructor? Do you know if a wedding license will cost you $30 or $300 in your out-of-the-country destination? If you have to scale back or settle for something less (say, get married by the little pond out back rather than on the sugary beach in Hawaii) would you be happy, or would you spend your wedding day with a chip on your shoulder? If it's the latter, you might be better off going the conventional route than trying to re-create a Hawaiian fantasy that only reminds you of what you couldn't have.

Know your audience. Sure, it's your day, but you should still be mindful of your guests. If the group, overall, veers toward conservative, steer away from something super far-flung. Save the Tarzan and Jane costumes for Halloween. Also be aware of the health of the special people involved in your wedding. It may be difficult for elderly parents or grandparents to get excited about an exhausting wedding fete in the Bahamas, or even to be physically able to traipse up a mountain. Do your attendants and family members really have the money to splurge on airfare and lodging? Your consideration of others will help make your day less stressful.

Get over the glamour. Before you get too smitten by the idea of a theme wedding or a destination wedding, think of the phrase "the grass is always greener." The enticing photos you see in resort brochures can be a big letdown once you get to the destination and discover that the beach is more rock than sand, for example. Give yourself a reality check before you throw away money on deposits and so forth.

Shopping

From negotiating deals to
you need to know

Smarts

securing contracts, here's what
before you hit the stores.

Aahh, shopping. It sounds so fun, so glamorous, so simple—until you realize it isn't just the fun stuff like trying on dresses and tasting cakes. There are venues to visit, photographers to find, and even insurance to consider. The typical wedding brings new meaning to the phrase shop 'til you drop. It can turn the most mild-mannered woman into Bridezilla or give an otherwise opinionated groom a severe case of "whatever-you-want-is-fine-with-me."

Haste makes waste, so lace up your running shoes. Getting your first choice in venues, florists, and photographers is a competition—after all, you aren't the only newly betrothed in town, and it's unlikely that caterers will be knocking at your door.

The Savvy Consumer

It doesn't really matter if you have a year to plan your wedding or just a few months. If you're not a smart shopper, you'll be sorry in the long run. "You need to think everything through, really use your head, and prioritize," wedding planner Erika Shay says. "If you think through each decision together carefully, you can spend a lot less money." Her top two rules: Try to negotiate a better price than what is first presented, and don't impulse buy. "Give yourself a little time to think about it," she says. "Always consult a friend, family member, or someone else to get a second opinion." Buyer's remorse is the last thing you need!

Before you hit the stores or pick up the phone to call potential vendors, develop a strategy. Consider these tips to keep budget blunders at bay:

Say charge it! As discussed in Chapter 1, you need to figure out how you're going to pay for things. If you're disciplined and pay off the full amount of your credit card bills each month, a credit card is usually the easiest way to go. Because you'll rack up deposit fees and charges faster than Julia Roberts' character fleeing the scene in **Runaway Bride**, it's a good idea to funnel expenses through one account. Using a designated credit card makes it easy to track where the money is going and also to dispute a charge if a deal falls through. Find a card that has incentives, such as frequent-flyer miles you can put toward your honeymoon. If your comfort level isn't high or your track record isn't good with charging things, figure out another payment method. (Refer to Chapter 1 for other options.)

Quiet the wedding bells. Don't get loose-lipped about "wedding" and "bridal" when you start talking to potential vendors or you begin your shopping spree. Often the price skyrockets at the mere mention that you need a limo to meet you after your "wedding" (versus you need a limo for an hour) or that you're looking for a place to hold a "wedding" reception (versus a "party for 50"). Obviously you have to spill the beans at some point, but try to save the details until later—and get the name of the person who quotes you the original price.

Know what "package deals" entail. In an effort to speed things up, many vendors will push their package deals. The best "package," though, may be one where you can cherry-pick different elements to create your own. Ask for that flexibility; it's unlikely the vendor will offer it without prompting. Compare the cost of the package deal versus choosing elements individually to see how much, if any, savings you're really getting. Similarly, compare the cost of the so-called wedding package to nonwedding packages. Make sure you know what's in each package; if you only look at the low-end package, you won't know what you're missing. "Go for the exclusive package, and then work backwards so you see what they're eliminating," wedding planner Jackson Lowell recommends.

Beware of hidden costs. If you've done your homework, asked the right questions, and read the fine print on contracts, there should be no such thing as hidden costs. Unfortunately even the most cautious couples can get tripped up by expenses they never imagined. (This may be when you wish you had budgeted for a wedding planner!) Don't assume that just because the ballroom you've chosen for your reception has chairs, they're free. The hotel may charge you anywhere from a couple bucks to $15 each to set them up. Other expenditures you may not be aware of: fees for a vendor to cut and/or serve cake (sometimes it's $4 or more per slice), corkage fees (even if you're allowed to bring in your own wine, you may get charged a fee for every bottle that's opened), overtime fees (for a facility, servers, and/or a musician), and "service" charges based on your per-guest count and added to the overall bill. Ask a lot of questions to avoid surprises. Borrow a journalistic rule: If someone tells you she's your mother, check it out. In wedding terms that translates into: If someone tells you they have chairs, ask how much they'll charge you to use them.

Get it in writing. If the vendor you're dealing with doesn't offer a contract, consider that a red flag. "It's very important to sign on the dotted line," Erika says. If you don't, you'll have little recourse if the caterer fails to show up or you arrive at the reception hall to find another couple already dancing away. Erika typically asks the couple to take the contract with them for 24 hours, read it over, and note any changes they'd like. Remember: A contract isn't a done deal until it's signed. "The worst thing the vendor can say is no," she says. "There's nothing you're going to ask for that has not been asked in the past. Don't get bullied."

Tread lightly in cyberspace. Like everything, online shopping has pros and cons. The upside is the convenience. The Internet is also a great research tool. You can scour bridal sites, look for floral arrangement ideas, and find a plethora of information without leaving home. The most obvious downside is that you can't see (other than a picture), feel, or touch what you're considering buying—so you don't know what you have until you get it. (Hopefully you get it in time for the wedding.) As such, use caution if you plan to buy online. Unless you're a risk-taker, limit your purchases to less-important items, such as attendant gifts, rather than ordering key items, such as dresses and bouquets. (See Chapter 4, page 133, for more about ordering attire online.)

The Venues

In real estate it's location, location, location. It's not that different with weddings. Where you choose to hold your ceremony and reception dictates the overall tone of the event and, of course, has a big impact on the bottom line. Do you dream of traipsing down a never-ending aisle with your train gracefully billowing behind? Churches book up fast, so get on the phone now. Perhaps you have your eye on a beautiful garden. Voilà! You've eliminated the cost of decorations, but tossed in the possibility of bad weather spoiling your special day. Maybe you're looking for a way to winnow the guest list without hurting someone's feelings; a destination wedding may be your ticket out of guiltdom.

Your planning can't really start until you select a wedding site. This venue drives so many decisions—the formality of the event, the number of attendants, the time of day, the food, the decorations or theme. Of course you can't shop for a site unless you have an idea of the number of guests you want to invite.

As discussed in Chapter 2, almost anything goes when it comes to venues. They run the gamut from the traditional church ceremony to a sky's-the-limit plunge from an airplane. Though the latter is reserved for those rarified daredevils, more conventional couples can take the path less traveled and still pull off a traditional, sophisticated ceremony. With a little sleuthing, you'll discover a wealth of possibilities that fits your budget. Consider these options, and also refer back to Chapter 2 for more alternative ideas:

Golden oldies. Mansions, living history farms, and other venues run by historical societies or nonprofit groups can often be rented. These settings tend to need minimal decorations. A quaint clapboard church on the premises may be your dream site and offer a way to incorporate a religious aspect in a nontraditional way.

Quick Tip Setting a budget involves more than crunching numbers. Your time is also a big investment, so budget that as well. Take a cue from professional organizers, who advise breaking big projects into more manageable chunks, such as 20 or 30 minutes a day. Set aside weekends for the more time-consuming projects. You'll thank yourself for the smaller progress you made during the week.

Natural instincts. A public or privately run park, garden, amphitheater, marina, boardwalk, or scenic area on a college campus lends itself naturally to weddings and receptions. Outdoor events, though, require a backup plan. Make sure there's a facility everyone can retreat to if Mother Nature doesn't cooperate. And just because a place is considered public doesn't mean there aren't restrictions or fees. Check city regulations and find out if there are festivals, parades, or other events already scheduled for the same day. The last thing you want is to be pledging your devotion while a marching band and fire-truck sirens provide background music.

Homeward bound. If simplifying is your mantra, everything you're looking for may be in your own backyard—or that of someone you know. A neighbor's rose garden, a relative's lakeside cottage, your parent's quiet country acreage, or a friend's condo clubhouse by the pool can create intimate and relaxed settings.

Double up. Pull maximum mileage from your venue—and budget—by choosing a site that works for both the wedding and the reception—a budget-savvy trick the wedding planners on **For Better or For Worse** often use. A hotel conference room can be dressed to the nines, then the makeshift walls can be

Where Is It?

You've figured out the "when," so now it's time to decide the "where." Consider the questions below to get general ideas on venues for your ceremony and reception.

• Do you envision a large wedding or a small one?

• What's your definition of large? What do you consider to be small?

• Is your wedding date set in stone, or are you willing to change it based on the availability of venues? Would you consider a nonweekend wedding?

• Is having the ceremony in a church or other religious site a must, or would you consider nontraditional sites?

• Are you concerned about how immediate family members or attendants would feel about a nontraditional wedding venue? Conversely, would key family members or attendants feel uncomfortable in the religious setting you're considering?

• Must the ceremony and reception take place on the same day?

• Do the ceremony and reception sites need to be close to your home and/or each other? Would you prefer that they be the same?

• In what mile radius do you want the ceremony and reception to be? Would guests, especially out-of-town ones, be able to find their way easily? Would the sites require special transportation?

• How long do you want the wedding ceremony to last? (Some churches may require a ceremony that lasts at least an hour.)

• Would you mind restrictions on the type of music allowed? (Some churches allow only preselected music and offer a list of what's acceptable.)

• Do you want all guests to be invited to both the ceremony and the reception? Or do you envision a small ceremony for relatives and close friends, followed by a larger reception—or vice versa?

• Do you want a full-blown reception, or even a reception at all? Would you prefer something simple, such as cake and punch in a church hall?

• Do you want the reception to begin immediately after the ceremony? If there's a lull between the two—for example, if you're taking photos after the ceremony—do you have something to occupy guests' time?

• Would you mind restrictions on bringing in your own food, alcohol, and/or servers?

• Are the sites you're considering large enough to accommodate your guests? Too large?

flung back to reveal the reception site. A country club may have an idyllic wedding spot on an outdoor patio overlooking lush greens and rolling hills, then guests can retreat indoors for the merrymaking. Museums, art galleries, and restaurants are other options.

Destination out of here. As discussed in Chapter 2, destination weddings continue to be wildly popular, but there are pros and cons that you need to really think through before locking yourself in. It may sound glamorous to get married on a tropical beach (and it is!), but there are lots of logistics, including legal issues, you'll encounter if you're getting married abroad. It may seem like you can cut costs because your guest list will be small, but you'll find that other expenses add up quickly. Do your research before you get your hopes set on a far-flung getaway; refer to Chapter 2 for more details.

Back to the basics. Remember city hall? That's the place many couples used to get hitched—and still can. If you choose a civil ceremony in a city hall or courthouse, you can save the hoopla for a reception, or skip it all together and let the money saved grow in your piggy bank. If your search for the perfect site leads you to the most basic but popular venue—a church, synagogue, or other house of worship—don't assume that you have the run of the place just because you or your parents are members. You face competition with other couples, holidays, other special events, and even with the weekly service. Book early and remember: There are no free lunches, not even at a church or other place of worship.

Take a Tour

Even if you've been dreaming of a specific site since you were a child or you've secretly been scouring places in recent months, an official visit to the venue is a must. You'll see things in a different light when you envision you and your guests in it. If the site is hundreds or more miles away, you should still see it before you commit, which means expenses for an extra trip need to be in your budget. If there's no way you can get there, you'll have to rely on photos, websites, and references, and hire a local wedding planner, event planner, or someone else to give you an unbiased scouting report.

Ask the Ceremony Site

Use these questions and the subsequent answers to help determine if the place you're considering for the ceremony fits your needs and budget.

• Is the date and time we selected available? Are there other events taking place there on the same day; if so, could those cause possible conflicts?

• What time of the day and days of the week can weddings be held at the site?

• What is the usage fee or donation that's expected? What other fees are there (i.e., for staff members, an officiant, musicians)?

• Can we bring in our own officiant or musicians?

• How many people does the location hold?

• Are there requirements pertaining to weddings, such as premarital sessions?

• Are there restrictions, such as on the religious affiliations of wedding participants? Music? Decorations? Where photographers can stand?

• What things will we have access to, such as an organ, a piano, candelabras, and an aisle runner?

• How soon can we have access to the site before the ceremony, and how soon after the event must we be out?

• Who is responsible for cleaning up after the ceremony?

• What rooms are designated as the dressing rooms? Where are the restrooms located?

• Can we control the air-conditioning, heating, and lighting?

• How much parking is available? Where can a limousine or other unconventional mode of transportation park in front of the venue?

• Will a representative from the venue be on-site during the ceremony to deal with any problems, such as improper ventilation? Is there an extra charge for such services?

• Is the site handicapped accessible? Can the elderly navigate the location easily?

• Is a deposit required? What's the cancellation policy?

• Is the site available for a rehearsal the day/evening before the ceremony? Is there a charge for this?

• If our ceremony is outdoors and there is inclement weather, what are our options?

Get the basic information about availability and fees over the phone, then save the rest for your visit. (See "Ask the Ceremony Site," page 83, and "Ask the Reception Site" **opposite** for a list of questions.) Never feel pressured to sign on the dotted line until all your questions have been answered to your satisfaction. To avoid wasting time, don't visit sites that aren't at the top of your list, unless it looks like you won't be able to secure one of your top choices. If possible, visit the venue at the time of day and the day of the week the event will be held to get an idea about lighting, noise level, traffic, and so forth. Additionally, consider these tips:

Book it. Though you shouldn't rush into a decision about the venue or venues, you shouldn't procrastinate either. Book the site six months to a year in advance, if possible; you may be surprised to find that superpopular places are booked three years in advance in some locales. The location dictates so many things about your wedding, so if nothing else, secure it, and then leave the rest of the planning until it gets closer to your wedding date.

One and done. You'll save money (and time looking around) if your ceremony and reception site are one in the same. Even the blandest hotel ballroom can be made ceremony-worthy with the right decorations (think arbors and candelabras that you can rent from florists and other places). Look for venues that make it possible to double up, such as a ballroom that has makeshift walls that can slide back to reveal the dining side, or a historical venue with an outdoor garden for the ceremony and a large dining hall for the reception.

No-cost catches. Don't let a "free" or "no-rent" site mislead you. The venue itself may be free, but you may soon discover that the cost of catering is ultrahigh and the tables, chairs, and silverware need to be rented. It's kind of like a movie theater that makes its money from the high-price concessions. Factor in all the mandates to determine if the "free" venue is really a bargain. If possible, give yourself at least 24 hours to think through all the pros and cons; you'll likely think of additional questions to ask the venue during that time too.

Ask the Reception Site

Before you commit to a venue for the reception, ask these questions, and make sure you're satisfied with the answers.

• Is the date and time we selected available? Are there other events taking place there on the same day, and could those cause possible conflicts?

• How many people does the location hold?

• What's the rental fee? What other fees are there? Is there an additional rental fee for tables, chairs, linens, and so forth? Is there a corkage fee for alcohol?

• Can we bring in our own caterers? Alcohol? Music? Servers?

• Do we have access to refrigerators? A stove? Where are the electrical sources? A microphone?

• When can we get access to the site to decorate, and when must we be out?

• Are there restrictions on the type of decorations?

• How much parking is available, and where is it? Is parking free? Where can a limousine or other unconventional mode of transportation pull up?

• Where are the restrooms?

• Will a representative from the venue be on-site during the event to deal with problems or questions? Is there an extra charge for this?

• Can we control the air-conditioning, heating, and lighting?

• How large is the dance floor? What type of flooring is it?

• Do we need to get any special permits, such as for serving alcohol? Is there a limit on amplified music (does it need to stop at a certain time)?

• Is the site handicapped accessible? Can the elderly navigate the location easily?

• Is the site insured? What does that cover?

• Who is responsible for cleanup?

• Is lodging available on-site? How many rooms are available, and what is the cost? Is there a wedding-package discount?

• Is a deposit required? What's the cancellation policy?

Invitations and Stationery

A trip to a stationery store can leave your head spinning. Who knew there was such a thing as a pew-seating card? What's the point of blank vellum inserts? Even if you're planning to make your own paper goods (there are some great projects designed by the **For Better or For Worse** wedding planners beginning on page 225), perusing the catalogs at a store that sells wedding invitations is a great starting point, a veritable treasure trove of free ideas on style and wording.

First, figure out what you need. Unless you're planning a fancy-pants event, you can skip the entrée choice cards and personal stationery and focus on these basics:

Save the date cards. For a destination wedding or any wedding with guests who need to book flights, these cards are common courtesy. Usually postcard style, the cards simply give the who, what, when, and where. To save costs it's fine to send the cards only to guests who need to make travel arrangements, but be aware that this could open a can of worms with closer-by guests who don't get a card and think that means they aren't invited. If money or time is an issue, just drop a plain postcard or a flyer done on your computer in the mail or send an e-mail. The important thing is to give people advance warning so they don't have to scramble to make travel arrangements or change their schedules upon receiving the invitation at a later date. Ideally send the cards six months before the wedding.

Invitations. The invitation is typically your first official contact with guests. In addition to spilling the details, the invitation should send a clear signal about the type of wedding you are planning. An engraved message in gold on off-white cardstock implies formal. A computer-generated invitation printed on Western-theme paper conjures up a laid-back casual gathering. Matching RSVP cards and maps usually accompany the invitations, though these can be done on your own to save costs. (If all your guests are already familiar with the location, a map may be unnecessary, saving you time and postage.) If you plan to invite some people to the reception but not the wedding, or vice versa, you'll need invitations for those as well.

Wedding ceremony programs. At a minimum this program gives a blow-by-blow of the wedding and names the key players. Some couples also use the program to thank their families and friends, to share stories of how they met, or to give their new address. Like invitations, the programs should match the tone of the wedding.

Thank-you cards. Purchase or make thank-you cards early on so they're at your fingertips when the wedding is over. If you're really on the ball, begin writing thank-you notes for gifts you receive before the wedding or addressing envelopes for ones you're sure will come in. Don't fret if the cards don't match the invitations and programs. Purchased packs from a discount store are fine, as are plain sheets of white or cream stationery. The important thing is to show your gratitude—and to do it in a timely manner.

In all cases, stationery is an area where it's easy to scale back without sacrificing style. For example, choose standard sizes of invitations and thank-you cards to avoid paying more for paper, odd-size cuts, or postage. Skip the nonessentials that suck up money and assemblage time, such as liner papers and foil-embellished envelopes that tuck inside the outer envelope (write all guests' names on the outer envelope). Put as much information as possible on the wedding invitation (but steer clear of crowded and tacky), including reception details, to avoid the need for a separate reception card. RSVP cards or even thank-you notes can be as simple as a no-envelope-needed postcard. Envision yourself as a guest: Do you want to have to wade through multiple envelopes and inserts to get to the important stuff—and doesn't that sound eerily similar to sorting through bill stuffers to get to the bill itself?

Know the Lingo

The wide world of invitations and ceremony programs can be like alphabet soup, with store clerks seemingly speaking a foreign language. Get vested in verbiage when you're ready to talk stationery. Here are some terms to know:

Engraving. This is considered the crème de la crème of printing processes, and it has the price tag to show for it. Letters are "stamped" from the back of the paper, leaving a depression that raises the letters on the front. The raised

Etiquette Says ...

• **Save the date cards:** Mail them six months before the event. Not possible? Skip snail-mail and pick up the phone to let faraway guests know key details. Even an e-mail message is better than someone receiving an invitation that requires them to scurry to make transportation plans.

• **Invitations:** Mail to guests one to three months before the event. Allow four to eight weeks for ordering. You don't have time to wait for your order to be processed? Generate your own from your computer printer. No time to handwrite the addresses? Enlist the help of a family member. A handwritten note is more personal than a computer-generated label.

• **Thank-you cards:** Buy them when you purchase invitations (or make them yourself); mail them within a month of opening each gift. An e-mail is not acceptable.

letters are printed with ink; gold is a popular choice for the most formal of gatherings. Unless you're looking to blow some cash, there's no need to splurge on engraving.

Thermography. Consider this the great imposter to engraved invitations. You'll get the raised-letter effect but at about half the cost of engraving.

Calligraphy. To elevate your invitations (or at least the addresses) to an art form, this fancy lettering fits the bill. You can hire a calligrapher (pricey and time-consuming) or choose computer-generated calligraphy, which is becoming more common. In general, calligraphy has a more formal feel.

Offset printing. Nothing fancy here. This is printing at its rawest: flat letters on paper. The advantage of this common method is that it's the least expensive, and you can choose multiple ink colors. (More ink colors will cost more money, though; simple black, chocolate brown, or deep forest green on white paper are always in vogue.) Font choices are nearly limitless, so you can select a more ornate one for a formal wedding or one that has a "let's party" feel for a casual ceremony. Wedding-invitation companies don't typically do this form of printing, so you may need to find your own print shop.

Laser printing. The trusty machine next to your computer may have everything you're looking for. You can whip up your own invitations or wedding programs without having to wait weeks or even months. You'll likely need to use lighter-weight paper to avoid jams. (Test various weights to see what will work best for your particular printer.) Many office-supply stores stock preprinted invitations set up on 8½×11-inch sheets of paper with perforations to separate the individual invitations. (See "Do-It-Yourself Stationery" on page 92 for alternatives to store-bought invitations and other stationery needs.)

Choosing the Words

Even though you could bury yourself with samples of differently worded invitations from catalog companies, putting pen to paper requires thought. Should you request the "honour" of someone's presence or the "honor"? Should parents be listed, and, if so, should they be before or after you and your mate?

Quick Tip Get a second and third set
of eyes to proofread your invitation and wedding program.
Do-overs are expensive and stressful! After a thorough
goings-over, put the process in reverse and read each piece
from the end to the beginning. This will force you to read
slower and prevent the eye from skipping over words that are
commonly grouped together.

The general guideline for verbiage is the more formal the affair, the more formal the wording (hence, the use of the British "honour"). Consider these guidelines as a starting point, and then tweak and bend the rules depending on the formality of your wedding.

Say when. For clarity always include the day, date, and year. Traditionally these are spelled out, such as Saturday, the Second of July, Two Thousand and Five. Times are also traditionally written out.

Proud parents. If you're including parents' names (a good idea, especially if they're helping with the expenses), use courtesy titles, such as Mr. and Mrs., for traditional invitations. In the most traditional invitations—back in the days when the bride's parents footed the bill—only the bride's parents were listed. Divorced or remarried parents require case-by-case consideration. A deceased parent is not typically listed.

Address the situation. Include the complete address of the ceremony site so there's no doubt what church or what park it is.

Religious rules. If you're having a religious ceremony, it's acceptable to reference that. You can invite guests to a "Christian celebration" or a "nuptial mass." Check with the officiant for the preferred wording for your denomination and affiliation.

Dos and don'ts. Though it's often not done, it's acceptable to include reception information on the invitation; you'll save costs in not having a separate reception card. Attire usually isn't mentioned, unless there's a compelling reason to do so, say either a black-tie affair or a very casual one. If you feel attire needs to be mentioned, add the information at the bottom of the invitation to save yourself the expense of a separate card. Never include information about where you registered or the type of gifts you'd like.

Sample Wording

Compare and contrast the following invitations and use them as a guide for selecting the wording that best suits the tone of your wedding.

Formal Invitation

Mr. and Mrs. John Doe
and
Mr. and Mrs. Robert Smith
request the honour of your
presence at the marriage of
their children
Peggy Ann Doe
and
Brent Joseph Smith
on Saturday, the Second of July
Two Thousand and Five
at Three O'clock
First Presbyterian Church
Five Twenty-Five Aspen Drive
Anytown, Arizona

Informal Invitation

John and Patricia Doe
and
Robert and Jean Smith
invite you to the marriage
of their children
Peggy Ann
and
Brent Joseph
on Saturday, July 2, 2005
at 3:00 p.m.
First Presbyterian Church
525 Aspen Drive
Anytown, Arizona

Do-It-Yourself Stationery

If you're looking for a way to personalize your special day and save some money in the process, make your own invitations, wedding programs, and other stationery items. With computers and printers at the ready, this once unheard of option is becoming commonplace. Granted it will take time, but it's one of the few DIY options that you can accomplish before the last minute when your nerves may be on the verge of fraying.

To figure out if you want to dive into the stationery business, get a few estimates on what the easy way would cost. You might decide that a few hundred bucks to have someone else handle everything is money well spent. Consider your guest list too. If your vision of handmade invitations requires handiwork, such as punching holes and looping ribbon through to tie into bows, you might go stir crazy with 200-some invites. If you're inviting 50 guests, that's another story.

You'll find inspiration by looking through sample invitations and programs in store catalogs. A crafts or hobby store that sells scrapbooking or rubber-stamping supplies is also a treasure trove of ideas. Consider these ideas too:

Enlist a friend. If you know someone who's a great scrapbooker, a graphic designer, calligrapher, or simply has a creative eye, ask if he or she is willing to help out. Your friend may even offer to handle the entire thing as a wedding gift to yours truly.

Take a test run. Before committing to do-it-yourself paper goods, do your homework. Check out the fonts on your computer to see if there's one you like and that fits the tone of your wedding. Run various types and weights of paper through your printer to see if the printer jams and to test printing quality. If you need to print on both sides, flip over the paper and run it through on the backside to check the quality. If the paper will be cut after printing, call around to copy centers to see what they charge for that (nothing screams penny-pinching-homemade more than crooked edges). If you end up having to buy new fonts, clip art, and so forth, the costs will add up in a hurry.

Start early. There's no need to wait until the bitter end to get going. Set up your design and worry about filling in the details, such as the name of the organist, later. You'll be a much happier couple toward the end if you don't have the wedding program or thank-you cards hanging over your heads.

Have fun. The wedding program is your chance to tell your story and show your personality. Some couples have included baby photos on their program, along with a story of how they met. A journalist's wedding program can be set up like a newspaper story, complete with a dateline; a pilot's can be presented in a ticket-style holder like an airline would give out. Such approaches make for riveting reading for seated guests, but if they don't fit the feel of your wedding, don't feel compelled to do something out of the ordinary.

Photography

Wedding planner Angie Bloom Hewett learned the importance of a good photographer the hard way. Her husband handled hiring the photographer and videographer for their wedding, and he went the low-cost route. "We got awful pictures," she says. "I never to this day will let him live it down. It was all a waste of time."

Indeed there are lots of areas where you can pinch pennies when you tie the knot—say, skip the bows on pews or nix the lemon filling on the cake. Photography isn't one of them. Ten years from now, the cake will be long forgotten, the flowers wilted, the dress boxed up or even sold. Pictures? They're forever. "Those are your memories," Angie says.

Quick Tip Designate a friend or family member as your official "unofficial" photographer. The person can snap photos while the photographer is changing rolls of film, as well as look out for candids, so you'll get a glimpse of things without having to wait for the real thing. Also choose a trusted friend or relative who has a keen eye—and who's not in the wedding party—to look for uneven lapels, out-of-place-hair, and so forth during photography.

Ask the Photographer

A picture may be worth a thousand words, but you won't be smiling if the photography bill is double what you expected. Ask these questions to find the right photographer.

• How long have you been in business? Is photography your full-time job?

• What's your specialty?

• How many weddings have you photographed in the past year? Past five years?

• How large have the weddings you've photographed been? What different types of settings have you photographed weddings in? Churches? Outdoors?

• Do you shoot in both color and black and white? Which is your specialty? Is there a difference in price between the two?

• What are your fees? What's included in that? Do you have a base rate? Do you charge by the hour, and is there a minimum number of hours? Do you charge for travel?

• Do you require an assistant? If so, who pays for that? What is the charge?

• What type of packages do you offer? What's included (i.e., the number of prints, is an album included)? Can we customize any of the packages?

• How many photographs will you take?

• How much time do we need to allot for you to take the photos?

• Do you prefer taking photos before or after the wedding? Are you willing to take location photos, such as at a nearby park? Will you scout additional portrait locations to find the best setting?

• Do you use digital camera equipment or traditional? Do you have lighting equipment?

• Can we purchase negatives if we want? If so, what's the cost? If not, how long do you keep them? What's the cost for getting prints made down the road? If you use a digital camera, can we get a disk with the photos?

• Do you take reception photos? How long will you stay?

• Will you provide a list of poses you plan to take? Can we specify certain poses we do or don't want and offer our ideas?

• Do you allow family members or other guests to snap some photos after you set up the poses?

• How long after the wedding will we have the proofs? The actual photos we order?

• Will you provide a contract we can review and sign?

• Can we see your portfolio? Can we see proofs from a recent wedding?

• Can you provide references from recent weddings?

And they don't come cheap. Photo costs vary wildly, but can easily run $3,000 or more. You can contain costs by keeping the number of photos to a minimum. If you're the type who freezes in front of the camera, it might be a good idea to scale back anyway. And, yes, it's better to scale back with a good photographer than to get a full package from a bad photographer.

If you decide to risk using an amateur, such as a shutterbug friend or college student, don't skimp on film. Load him or her up and ask the person to shoot away so you'll be bound to have some keepers. Amateurs usually don't have the fancy equipment and lighting a pro has, so regardless of how talented the person is, you won't get a truly professional look. But, hey, that may be perfectly fine. If it's a casual wedding in a park, you might prefer a more natural look anyway.

Before making appointments with potential photographers, figure out what style of photos you want. Black and white photographs are making a comeback. This photo-journalistic style is artsy and dramatic (and tends to cost more than color). Often a couple chooses a combination of color and black and white photos. Decide if you want traditional poses (think bride and groom at the altar, bride and groom surrounded by wedding party at the altar) or more casual ones—perhaps of you and your new spouse in a rowboat heading out to the middle of a pond that's on the premises.

You also need to agree on the extent to which you want the event documented. Make a list of what you two consider to be essential and nonessential photos. In the long run, a portrait of you together and one of the two of you surrounded by family will be more valued than ones of the groom pretending to fling the garter. Cut out some of the cheesiness, and the "Say cheese!" part will be easier to digest moneywise.

Photography Logistics

Before you eagerly sign on the dotted line with a photographer whose photos you've fallen for, impose a waiting period. Make sure you're both truly comfortable with the person, not just with his or her work. Did the person put you at ease on the phone or in your meeting? Did you laugh, or was it all serious stuff? If the photographer lets his or her stress show on the big day, it will naturally latch onto you. Professionals remain cool, calm, and collected, even when the flash isn't working or rain clouds are forming.

You also need to determine if you want the photos taken before or after the ceremony—or both. If you want to take the photos before the wedding, is there another event scheduled that day that would conflict with this? Would the sun be sunk and too dark for outdoor photos, or would it be high noon and you'd be squinting in every frame? If you wait to take photos after the wedding, would guests get weary of waiting at the reception?

The venue you've chosen for the ceremony may also dictate what can and can't be done in terms of photography. Some places have restrictions on where the photographer can stand during the ceremony, or they may even prohibit photography or the use of a flash during the ceremony. Does the schedule you and the photographer talked about work with the officiant and/or ceremony site? To avoid conflicts on the day, ask now.

Remember the Video

Photos aren't the only way to document your wedding and reception. Videography has become standard practice. Virtually the same rules apply to choosing a videographer as they do to choosing a photographer. Chief among them is that you get what you pay for. You can assign a relative to run the camcorder or you can hire a steady-handed professional. The latter is expensive, and may be out of the question—so have a friend start reading up on the dos and don'ts of running a camcorder. A middle ground is to find a college student who's studying in this area or see if a cameraperson at a local television station moonlights as a wedding videographer.

Review the guidelines and questions already mentioned for photographers when seeking a videographer. (Check the directory of your phone book, and ask around to get references from friends and other people. Your photographer may be able to recommend someone too.) Of course, you'll want to view sample tapes to assess the quality.

To reduce costs if you're hiring someone, limit what he or she tapes. Limit it to the ceremony, for example, so you're not paying someone to stick around until midnight. No one really wants to sit through a five-hour tape anyway.

One thing that is different with video is that you can have the videographer edit and add graphics, still photos, or voice-overs so you end up with a mini movie of your day, or even from childhood on. You'll pay more for those types of extras. If you're strapped for cash now, go with the basic footage and hire a company down the road to add the extras. The question about what to give as your first anniversary present is solved!

The Food

When the big day rolls around, you and your betrothed will be pledging your undying devotion. The guests? They'll be thinking about the food. Consider it a cold, hard fact that the way to your guests' heart is through the stomach. The food will get guests talking, and it's your chance to show that you're thinking of them. (Turn to Chapter 6, page 176, for more about the importance of food and to Chapter 8, page 205, for a menu/food planning worksheet.)

The time of your reception obviously dictates what you serve. Hungry tummies don't want to munch on pastries at 7 p.m., nor do they want a plate piled with pasta at 10 a.m. If you're a smart couple, you've chosen a reception time that works with your budget. Generally hosting a breakfast or brunch is less expensive than a dinner, and a buffet is less expensive than a sit-down dinner (though that can vary if people go back for seconds and thirds).

So what can you do to ensure that guests eat, drink, and be merry? Regardless of the entrées or munchies you want to serve, it all boils down to finding the right person for the job. Before you start the search for the caterer and the all-important cake baker (even if they end up being you and your family!), have an idea of what you want by answering these questions:

What's your style? Two conventional choices are a sit-down meal or a buffet-style serving line, but the options don't end there. A cocktail-style reception with hors d'oeuvres can be a less-costly alternative that's still elegant and satisfying; these are especially nice for midafternoon or off-hour weddings where guests won't be expecting a main meal. Brunches are another option, with morning weddings becoming popular with many couples. A potluck where immediate family members bring in the goods is a down-home, budget-friendly alternative to the expected. Barbecues or picnics are great for casual outdoor affairs.

Where's your reception? If you've signed on to a package deal at a hotel or other venue, you may not have much of a say in how things are served, and you may have only a limited say in what's served. If not, you'll need to factor in the venue. Does it have adequate facilities for the type of food you want to serve? If not, can you rent roasters, heating plates, or small refrigerators? Is the overall feel of the venue suited to the style of food you'd like? Serving prime rib to guests seated at a picnic table in a park would seem awkward, as would offering ham sandwiches and chips at a prestigious members-only country club.

What's the desired ambiance? If the overall tone of your wedding is formal, skip the bowls of popcorn and pretzels. A sit-down meal or fancy appetizers for a cocktail-style reception are more in order. Serve-yourself-whenever buffets have a more casual feel to them, though adding carving stations for meats fancies up the everyday buffet.

How much variety do you want? Multiple entrée options or a plethora of appetizers gets costly. You can easily simplify without seeming cheap. One thing you may need to factor in, though, is vegetarians. Have at least one option everyone can enjoy. If you're serving a sit-down meal, many caterers suggest allotting 10 percent of the total number of guests for a vegetarian alternative.

What's the time frame? You've probably already figured out by now that good people book up fast. If you're planning a quickie wedding, you might need to get creative in your meal planning. Factor in the length of time you have access to the venue too. If you've hired someone who needs five hours of setup time, but you can only get into the venue two hours in advance, you've got a problem.

Finding the Foodies

The safest way to ensure that the meal goes off without a hitch is to hire a professional caterer. A pro knows how to run the show: how to time the food so it's just right, how to present it, how to serve it, how to prevent guests from getting food poisoning. Ask around for the names of caterers and check the phone book. If you like the meal or appetizers served at an office party or special reception you attend, ask for the caterer's name. Colleges that offer culinary programs are another outlet.

By all means, though, you can take a road less traveled and pull off a personalized reception. An Italian or Indian restaurant may be just the place to cater authentic foods that celebrate your heritage—a smart idea the wedding planners on **For Better or For Worse** often use to serve up meals that complement the theme or style of the event they're planning. A clambake on the beach or hot dogs roasted over a campfire offer old-fashioned fun. Remember it never hurts to ask; the people may be flattered that you're interested in having them help you out on your big day.

Expert Advice **When looking for vendors, get recommendations from people you know and try to choose vendors who are familiar with the venues you've booked. "I find that there's a lot more cohesion at the function when vendors have been referred by other people or they're familiar with the location," wedding planner Sally Steele says.**

Ask the Caterer

Good food starts with a good caterer, be it your Aunt Gertrude, the grocery-store deli, or a hotel staff. Use these questions to help find the right person for the job.

- What's your specialty?

- Can we see sample menus and photos of your presentation?

- Can we taste samples?

- What's your catering experience? Did you train at a culinary institute? Where?

- What style do you prefer? Buffet? Sit-down meal?

- How many weddings have you done in the past year? Past five years? What's the average size of the weddings you've catered?

- Do you have a license? Insurance?

- What do you charge and how do you charge? Per plate? Per person? Do you itemize the charges?

- Do your charges include gratuity? If so, for whom does this cover? Is there an extra delivery charge?

- What do your charges entail? Are servers included? Are there extra fees for such things as linens, silverware, or chairs?

- Will your servers be able to cut cake? Pour champagne? Is there an additional charge for these?

- Do you stick to your own menu or will you customize and make something we're interested in?

- Do you cook at the venue or off-site? Do you need access to kitchen facilities?

- What do you do in terms of setup the actual day? Do you set the tables or do you only set up the serving area?

- How involved are you with the planning and the execution? Will you be available for questions? If not, who will the contact be? Who will be the primary contact the day of the event?

- How many staff will you have at the event? Are they professionals?

- How much time to you require for setup? Cleanup?

- How long before the reception do you need a head count? How much flexibility is there to change it after we give you a number?

- How many extra meals do you plan for above the head count? Who is charged for that?

- Do you have other events scheduled for the day of our wedding? What about the days before or after?

- Will you provide a contract for us to review and sign? Do you require a deposit? What is your cancellation policy?

Restaurants. A favorite restaurant, whether fancy or down-home, may be your ticket to a great meal. Rent out a diner that serves malts and burgers, and you'll get a fun venue and food rolled into one package. Even if a restaurant doesn't rent its facilities or offer catering services for off-site events, don't cross it off your list. Check the carryout menu; you might be surprised to find that many restaurants offer large-size portions to feed 10, 20, or even 50. A relative or friend can swing by to pick up tins of pasta or barbecue that you can serve to guests.

Commodity and nonprofit groups. Organizations whose sole purpose is to promote their products—be it beef, lamb, or turkey—are usually accustomed to serving large groups and might cut you a good deal. Ask a local or county egg council if it's willing to whip up omelets for a brunch, or find out if the pork producers' group will grill chops. Similarly, a city's parks and rec department that can be hired out for children's birthdays or other events might be able to adapt its offerings to your smaller group of guests. Or a church group known for its great fund-raiser dinners may be willing to re-create the menu for your reception.

Grocery stores. Whether you want the basic meat-and-cheese platter or a full-fledged meal, today's supermarkets offer an ever-expanding catering menu. Most grocery stores also have bakeries, so you have one-stop shopping for the meal, cake, and drinks.

Tearooms. Don't rule out a quaint tearoom because the venue is too small. The operator may be willing to take his or her show on the road and bring the food to you. Similarly, someone who runs a bed-and-breakfast and is used to fixing meals for others may be a worthy candidate.

Friends and relatives. Sometimes the best people for the job are in your inner circle. You can save money preparing and serving the food on your own. However, it takes special planning and preparation to do it; see "Menu Matters," page 107, for tips. (continued on page 104)

All About Cakes

No wedding-day celebration is complete without a sweet treat. Though any dessert will do—including cookies and pies—cakes are still the most popular option.

Frosting Factoids

Don't fret if you don't know ganache from gum paste. This glossary will familiarize you with common cake terms before you go knocking on a baker's door.

- **Basketweave (or latticework):** A decorative technique that creates the look of a woven basket.

- **Buttercream:** The traditional creamy frosting. Can be colored or flavored as desired. Melts in the sun or high heat.

- **Cornelli:** A decorative technique that yields a lacy pattern.

- **Dotted Swiss:** A decorative technique that creates a dotted pattern, comparable to dotted Swiss fabric.

- **Fondant:** A sugary paste that is rolled out very thin and then placed over the cake to create an ultrasmooth, sleek surface.

- **Ganache:** A relatively thick chocolate concoction that can be used either as icing or filling.

- **Gum paste:** A thick mixture used for decorations. Though edible, gum paste is not as tasty as a traditional frosting.

- **Marzipan:** A ground-almond paste that can be used for decorations or rolled out like fondant and used as an icing.

- **Piping:** The process of using a pastry bag to apply icing.

- **Royal icing:** A type of frosting commonly used for the piping, flowers, and other decorations. It's piped from a pastry bag. Royal icing hardens as it dries.

Common Cake Styles

Wedding cakes can take many forms, from multitiered masterpieces to simple single-layered confections. Here's a look at some of the options.

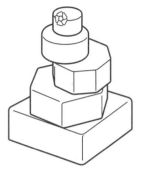

- **Single-layer:** A cake of any shape (round, square, rectangular, or multisided, such as pentagon) set on its own base.

- **Multilayer (no columns):** Individual cakes of any shape stacked one on top of the other.

- **Multilayer (with columns):** Individual cakes of any shape stacked one on top of the other; columns support the layers.

- **Individual desserts:** Small desserts—including petits fours, cupcakes, and doughnuts—placed on top of one another to resemble a traditional cake.

The Cake

If you think choosing a baker is a cakewalk, it's time to come down from your sugar high. Back in the good old days, the choices were black (as in chocolate) and white. Today's wedding cakes have slipped into a gray area, with tempting choices on flavors, fillings, toppings, frostings, and more. And every upgrade (think fondant, lemon filling, and a scoop of sorbet) is followed by the cha-ching of the cash register. A fancy-schmanzy cake can cost thousands of dollars. Even a basic confection can run $300 or more.

Whether it's a towering tiered sensation covered with smooth-as-silk fondant and piped with realistic-looking roses or a two-layer cake from Mom's oven, the cake is the pièce de résistance of your reception. More than just a calorie-laden indulgence, it's a decorative focal point and a time-honored tradition. Skip the cake (or at least fail to offer some form of sweet treat) and you run the risk of a riot. Of course, you may have different ideas about the importance of a cake. It's your wedding, and you know your budget and priorities.

Don't apologize if your wedding fund or your priorities lead you to basic chocolate and white with buttercream frosting. You can pick up a tasty one from a grocery-store bakery. If you have your sights set on a special cake, start the search for a baker early—about six to eight months before the wedding. Some bakers

Ask the Baker

Apply the same questions to potential bakers that you did for caterers; see page 100. Additionally find out these answers:

• How much cake should we order based on the number of guests we've invited? What size of slices does this allow for?

• Do you charge a rental fee for tiers or other items? What other additional costs are there, such as any transportation fees for bringing the cake to the site?

• Do you take special steps to ensure the top tier of the cake can be frozen and edible on our first anniversary? (If you want to follow this tradition, some bakers will add liquor to a portion of the cake or use other methods to help it withstand 12 months in the deep freeze.)

take on only a limited number of cakes, such as one or two a week because
baking and decorating a cake can be labor-intensive. Even if you're going the
grocery store route, there's no reason to wait until the last minute. At a minimum
you can get estimates to compare costs.

How can you have your cake and eat it too? Consider these budget-
friendly tips:

Go for the little guy. Instead of choosing a baker or bakery that specializes
in wedding cakes, opt for one that doesn't. The small mom-and-pop bakery
down the street (or, as we already mentioned, the grocery-store bakery) may
give your cake more personal attention because it's a fun departure from the
norm, and the cost is usually less.

Scale back. Opt for a smaller, simpler main cake and serve the majority of
guests less-expensive sheet cakes. Hold the fancy fillings and frostings and go
light on the labor-intensive decorations. Topping a cake with a few fresh flowers
may be decoration enough.

Nix the groom's cake. This standard-size cake that traditionally sits next to
the main cake is a fun way to get the guy involved (he can choose his own
flavor and style), but it's not a necessity.

Think less is more. You'll get more bang for your buck if you serve smaller
pieces. Ask your baker what size of slices he or she serves; if it's large, ask for it

to be reduced slightly—say from 4-inch cuts to 3-inch. (Even if the baker isn't serving the cake, most will "score" sheet cakes to give a cutting guideline, so be sure to discuss size in advance.) If you're serving a meal, a small slice will be enough to satisfy most guests' sweet tooth. If you have a cake-and-punch reception, serve larger pieces.

Bake it. If you or someone you know is an experienced baker, consider making your own cakes—but be forewarned that adding the finishing touches before the wedding is a chore the bride and groom shouldn't attempt, and there's no guarantee of the end result. You don't have to wait until the busy last few days before the wedding to make the cakes. Place unfrosted cakes in airtight freezer containers and put them in the freezer. A butter-type cake can be frozen up to four months; an angel, sponge, or chiffon cake can be frozen up to three months. Pop them out a day before the wedding to frost and decorate. Another alternative is to purchase less-expensive undecorated cakes from a bakery and add the embellishments yourself.

That said, don't feel compelled to serve the conventional stacked or tiered round cake. Cupcakes have shed their elementary-school image to become a trendy wedding dessert, tiered on pedestals. A square cake, or even one shaped to match your wedding theme or hobbies, is another welcome departure. Smaller cakes can be used as centerpieces on the guest tables—not only is it a convenience for guests who won't have to walk up to the cake table, but you've also cut out the cost of other centerpieces. If you really want to take a walk on the wild side, skip the cake for a mound of doughnuts, iced sugar cookies, tiers of cheesecake, or even pie. Guests may come to the reception expecting cake, but as long as they get their "just dessert" they'll feel satisfied—and will be talking about the break from tradition for days to come.

The Drinks

Many guests can take or leave the punch, but a bit of bubbly is another matter. The decision to serve alcohol can be a difficult one. Guests may get miffed about a cash bar, and nondrinking guests may not like the thought of alcohol at all. Plus, do you really want to end up with a bunch of inebriated guests? How you want to handle this topic is your call. (Turn to Chapter 6 for more on this subject.)

Check with your venue (especially if it's a city park or other public space) on any restrictions regarding alcohol and to make sure it has a liquor license. Find out what hidden costs there may be, such as corkage fees (which can be $25 or more a bottle). If you have to use the on-site bar service, you may want to have an open bar for only an hour or two, and then switch to a cash bar. A morning wedding, of course, solves the dilemma almost entirely—though even some early-rising well-wishers may still enjoy a champagne toast. Offer orange juice or sparkling fruit juice for nondrinkers and children.

If the venue allows you to bring your own alcohol and serve it yourself, you'll save costs. Purchase the items well in advance to avoid adding it to your last-minute to-do list. Ask for bulk discounts or buy what's on sale. You can control costs (and the amount guests have to drink) by serving champagne only during a toast, not throughout the entire event. Limiting the selection to beer and wine, rather than mixed drinks, also reduces costs.

Serving alcohol carries responsibility with it too. If you know your guests will want to whoop it up, hold the reception within walking distance of the hotel where guests will stay. Or plan to hire a transportation service or call a cab.

Menu Matters

As you begin to think about menus and look around for caterers and bakers, you may just decide to do it on your own. As mentioned previously, it takes special planning and preparation—which escalates by the number of guests. Appoint a food committee of trusted (and willing) friends and relatives and assign one person as your cochair so there's a definite leader who knows what's going on. On the day of the event, the cochair moves into the solo chairperson spot. You won't have time to fill the person in on the details or worry about whether the icing is melting in the sun, so your cochair needs to be "trained" and clued-in in advance about all details. Be sure to test recipes. Pay attention to how long it took to prepare and cook the item, not just its taste.

Regardless of whether you decide to do it yourself or hire a caterer or baker, there are a few common threads that will make your life easier and keep costs down. Consider these tips to help you make sound choices.

- Buffets are popular for their ease. Skip the expensive carving stations and opt for a buffet where guests can serve themselves. If doing it yourself, use roasters to keep sliced meats or vegetables hot.

- If you don't have the confidence to tackle the cake, find a baker who's willing to make and frost the cake, but skip the decorating part, which can add greatly to the bill. You can easily add a cake topper, a few fresh flowers on the tiers or at the base, or even edible glitter to dress it up.

- Keep in mind the food hierarchy when choosing main entrées: Chicken (and sometimes seafood, depending on the locale) is typically less expensive than beef or pork.

- To save on alcohol costs, look for ways to stretch the more-expensive elements of a drink—á la spiking the punch back at the prom.

- Don't go overboard on appetizers. If you reduce the offerings from six to two, guests will never be the wiser.

- Typically children eat less than adults, so ask if your caterer will give you a break for a designated number of kids' meals. You'll likely need to negotiate this before you actually know how many kids will attend. Don't get hung up on the exact number; you're looking for more of a goodwill gesture and a little break from the caterer.

- Skip the cheese tray, which typically is the biggest source of leftovers.

- If you plan to serve wine, contact a winery directly to see if it will give a bulk discount in return for the publicity of being the featured winery.

- When choosing a cake, focus on the taste, not looks. You can awe guests with a beautiful cake, but if they have to choke it down because it's dry and tasteless, that's what they'll remember.

- Load up on the carbs. Pasta dishes tend to be less expensive than meat entrées. Meatless pasta dishes offer an option for vegetarians.

- Simplify! Take the path of least resistance whenever possible. Punch that requires ice cream, for example, is more high-maintenance and costly than a basic fruit punch.

Music or Entertainment

I f you decide to have music at your reception, you've made a good choice. It's a great way to set the mood and get the party going. When deciding what type of music to have, consider more than your personal tastes. You may love dusting to Madonna or pumping iron to Billy Ocean, but that may not be appropriate for a wedding reception. Find a band or DJ that fits the desired ambiance or the earnest nature of an event. If it's a Sunday brunch, a small instrumental group may be the ideal way to provide background music. If your guest list is heavy on older friends or relatives, a big band may get people up on their feet.

Not very creative, you say? How about having strolling violinists roam the room, a small jazz ensemble provide background music, or a barbershop quartet perform on the half hour? A cousin with a great voice or the vocalist from your ceremony can record a favorite tune (or give a live rendition) for your first dance. Look for low-cost musicians within your inner circle, or call a local symphony or other musical group to check on the costs and availability of some of their musicians.

Turn to Chapter 6 for more about the reception music (Chapter 5 touches on ceremony music). The following covers what you need to know about hiring different types:

Live band. A band is usually more costly than a DJ and can sometimes steal the show (courteous guests may want to watch the band rather than mingle). Depending on the band, it can bring a certain "upscale" flair to the reception. A jazz ensemble, for example, can really set the mood. You obviously need to hear the band before hiring it, and keep in mind that a band will be more limited in its musical selections than a DJ. To save money you might be able to hire a member or two of the band to perform at the wedding ceremony. A trumpet player, for example, can duck out of the reception venue while the rest of the group is setting up to toot his or her horn for the processional.

Disc jockey. The biggest advantage of a DJ is the wide variety of music he or she can play. You can create a song list that caters to young and old. DJs are typically less expensive than a live band (though a bad band may be cheaper, and that may be a sign of the quality). Often the DJ acts as emcee of the reception. As such you need to choose wisely. You don't want an ill-mannered DJ ruining your event. A DJ can cost $400 or up, depending upon your locale. Skip the light show or fancy extras to save money.

Other entertainer. Who says you have to go the traditional route and provide music? Entertainment comes in many forms—a casino, a carnival, mimes. Refer to Chapter 2 and Chapter 6 for ideas to put a unique spin on your reception and merriment.

Ask the Band or DJ

Bands and DJs book up fast, but there's no reason to commit to one you're unsure about. Ask these questions before you book the gig.

• What type of music do you specialize in? Can we see your play list or song book?

• How many wedding receptions have you done in the past year? Past five years?

• What do you charge? How many hours is that good for?

• Are you accustomed to being the emcee of the reception?

• Do you charge for travel? How much?

• What type of equipment do you have? What setup requirements are there?

• How much time do you need to set up?

• How often do you take breaks, and for how long? What do you play during breaks?

• If we want you to play longer, what overtime fees do you charge?

• Do we have flexibility in when we want you to play? For example, if we don't want background music during the cocktail hour, will we get a reduced price?

• What size of group are you used to playing for? What size of a room are you used to playing in?

• Do you have an upcoming event we can hear you at?

Whatever route you go, make sure you understand exactly what the charges are and for how long. If the party is hopping, and you ask the DJ or band to stick around for an extra 30 minutes, you may end up paying a pretty penny in overtime charges for both the entertainment and the venue.

The Flowers

Here's something you won't hear often during the planning stage: Take a deep breath ... relax. Why? Finding a florist is something you can put toward the bottom of your list. That's not to imply that the flowers aren't important, but they're something you can delay until after the sites are secured and the dresses are ordered. In fact, you should delay your selection until you've settled on key elements. The style and colors of the wedding party's garb, as well as the overall tone of the wedding, for example, affect the types and styles of flowers you choose. Heck, if you're really thinking about saving on the flowers, book the event in a garden.

If you time it right, you won't have to spend much on flowers. Churches, restaurants, and historical facilities, for example, are often decorated with poinsettias and fresh trees around Christmas or lilies at Easter. Keep in mind, however, that the price of flowers rises around certain popular flower-giving holidays, such as Christmas and Valentine's Day.

Before shopping for a florist, look in your own backyard. If you can finagle some green-thumb or artistic friends to help out (you'll be too busy the hours leading up to your wedding), you might be able to pluck your own bouquets or centerpieces. (Turn to Chapter 9, page 209, for some easy-to-make, budget-friendly ideas from the **For Better or For Worse** wedding planners.) Even the wildflowers, grasses, and twigs growing along the roadside are yours for the taking. Freebie bouquets or centerpieces lend a fresh feel to a casual wedding and are great for a couple that loves the outdoors. Just make sure you don't nab a state flower or other off-limits specimen and end up answering to a judge. And steer clear of poison ivy!

Whether you do it yourself or hire it out, think things through before setting your mind on a certain bloom. Consider these tips:

Prioritize. Determine who and what gets flowers. (See "Flower Tally" **opposite**.) Do you want fancy floral arrangements at the altar and flowers on every pew? Would boutonnieres look silly on groomsmen dressed for a wedding in a barn? A bigger question: Do you even want flowers? Bouquets, at a minimum, seem like a given, but even those can be nixed for a pretty fan, single tapers, or even a family Bible. Table centerpieces can be a zesty basket of fresh fruit, a bounty of gourds, or a quirky goldfish in a bowl.

Fresh or fake? Though fresh flowers are always fashionable, you can sniff out some savings by using dried or artificial varieties. Not only do they cost less, but arrangements made of these alternatives can also be done well in advance of the event. Dried arrangements and bouquets are especially nice for a fall wedding. If fresh is a must, consider a combination of fresh and dried or artificial, or look for ways to scale back on the amount of fresh flowers needed.

Seasonal splendor. You'll pay less for flowers that are in season, so grab a gardening book and find out what those are. If you have an abundance of lilacs or lily-of-the-valley from the yards of relatives, you may have everything you need for a sprightly spring wedding. The danger, of course, is that they may not be at prime bloom when the wedding rolls around. Have a backup plan, even if that means a quick trip to the grocery-store floral department. If you must have a special flower shipped in, limit it to something special that will be noticeable, such as the bridal bouquet, which you'll see years from now in the photos.

Floral Fancies

Do you prefer flowers to be footloose and fancy-free or tightly coiffed? The style of bouquets and arrangements you choose should complement the overall tone of the wedding. Remember that centerpieces shouldn't interfere with conversation. Keep arrangements low to the table or tall and slim. Consider these tips for balancing the floral budget:

Go solo. Contrary to popular opinion, one isn't lonely. A single stem carried by each bridesmaid—or even the bride—is striking and impactful, as is a vase with just one flower. If you're going for the onesies, choose dramatic blooms such as a calla lily, gladiola, sunflower, or peony. A single rose, of course, is also effective, though more expected.

Think strategically. Think through the placement of the arrangements and where they'll be seen most. In a church, for example, all eyes are on the altar, so set the stage in that area and forget about the pews.

Show your green thumb. Potted plants are a great way to freshen up a setting—think mums in the fall, petunias in the summer. Large home centers and discount stores usually have a vast selection and great prices. You can give the plants as gifts for those who helped with the event. Green plants can also help fill in the gaps where needed. They can even stand on their own as

Flower Tally

Use this list to assess your floral needs and to ensure that you don't forget anyone or anything.

Bouquets
- [ ] Bride, for carrying
- [ ] Bride, for tossing
- [ ] Bridesmaids
- [ ] Flower girl

Others: _____

Total: _____

Boutonnieres
- [ ] Groom
- [ ] Groomsmen
- [ ] Ring bearer
- [ ] Ushers
- [ ] Fathers/grandfathers

Others: _____

Total: _____

Corsages
- [ ] Mothers/grandmothers
- [ ] Personal attendant

Others: _____

Total: _____

Ceremony Arrangements
- [ ] Entry
- [ ] Guest-book table
- [ ] Pews
- [ ] Altar

Others: _____

Total: _____

Reception Arrangements
- [ ] Entry
- [ ] Guest book/gift table
- [ ] Table centerpieces
- [ ] Food serving tables
- [ ] Cake
- [ ] Cake table

Others: _____

Total: _____

Ask the Florist

If you've added flowers to your shopping list, use these questions as a guide to getting what you want. A visit to a floral shop will also give clues to the quality. Check to see if the in-stock flowers are wilting (after all, those could end up at your wedding).

- How long have you been in business?

- What's your specialty? Can we see photos and samples of your work?

- How many weddings have you provided flowers for in the past year? Past five years?

- Where do you purchase your flowers? What will be in season and most widely available at the time of our wedding?

- Is there any discount for choosing in-season flowers?

- What is your style? Are you willing to create bouquets and arrangements based on magazine photos we provide?

- What size have the weddings you've done been?

- What are your fees? What's included in that? Do you charge rental fees for vases, candelabras, or other items?

- What type of packages do you offer? What's the cost?

- How fresh will the flowers be? How far in advance do you order them, so we'll know for sure that they're available and will be fresh?

- When will you deliver the flowers? Is there a delivery fee?

- Do you set up the arrangements at the venue?

- Do you have arrangements that can be rented?

- Have you provided flowers for our ceremony and/or reception sites before? If so, do you have photos of how they looked or ideas on decorating?

- How large is your staff? Who will be our contact? Who will be in charge the day of the event?

- Can you provide references from recent weddings?

- Do you have other events scheduled for the day before, the day of, or the day after our ceremony and reception that might conflict?

centerpieces: A few large hosta leaves or peace lily leaves placed in a small, clear glass vase makes a classy statement.

Put a twist on tradition. Everything doesn't have to come up roses at a wedding. Conventional wedding flowers, such as white roses, tulips, and gardenias, tend to be more expensive than other blooms. Find a flower or florist that will set your wedding apart from others. Big blooms, such as peonies and hydrangeas, can cover a lot of ground (fewer flowers means less money). Lily-of-the-valley is nice for simple, hand-tied bouquets.

Simplify. Like so many things in life, it's the cost of labor that adds up. To minimize floral charges, choose simple arrangements. Hand-tied bouquets, for example, are less costly than more elaborate ones requiring plastic holders—and they work for both formal and casual weddings.

Go off the beaten path. If your city has a wholesale floral shop, you can snag some good deals and have a great selection. Many discount and grocery stores also have a nice floral selection, usually at cheaper rates than a traditional florist. Get the names of people who sell flowers at a weekly farmer's market too; you might be able to strike a deal with them. (continued on page 118)

Flower Power

What's your style when it comes to bouquets? A florist will want to see fabric swatches of the dresses and likely photos—or at least a photo of the bridal gown—to offer ideas on proportion and color. Consider these common choices.

Arm bouquet: A grouping of long-stem flowers designed to be cradled in the arm, a la beauty pageant style. This type isn't functional if two people will escort the bride down the aisle.

Cascade: A traditional bridal bouquet with flowers that cascade down from the main portion.

Hand-tied bouquet: A simple arrangement of flowers with stems left intact and tied together with ribbon.

Nosegay: A cluster of flowers, sometimes arranged on a round plastic holder. Typically the flowers are small and varied; a nosegay can require several dozen flowers. The stems are usually wrapped with ribbon.

Round bouquet: A ball-shape floral arrangement, which is usually placed in a plastic holder.

Single flower: Simple and classy; a single stem of any flower can be carried by the bride or female attendants.

Wrist corsage: A flower or grouping of flowers outfitted with a band and worn around the wrist. Wrist corsages have reemerged as a popular option for bridesmaids and other female wedding party members.

Consider color. White flowers are sophisticated and are a symbol of purity, and many white flowers emit wonderful fragrances. Depending upon the type of white bloom, it takes more of them to make an impact (especially if you're using them for centerpieces placed on tables with white linens). White flowers also are less forgiving of wilting, showing brown edges more readily than other colors. As such, don't be afraid to add a jolt of color to the setting with a bright bloom that complements the wedding scheme.

Rent them. If you've awed at a stage or special-events tent that was dressed to the nines, you might be surprised to find out the beauty came from renting. Ask a florist or special events planner if you can rent bouquets, greenery, and vases. Alternatively, borrow items that can be used as vases and/or pots from family and friends to save money—Mom's pitcher collection, one favorite piece from your closest friends, and so forth.

Pull double duty. Get maximum mileage out of the flowers you do choose. The bridal and bridesmaids bouquets can serve as decorations for the cake table. Transport flowers used at the wedding to the reception site. (If the florist doesn't do this, you'll need to arrange for someone else to.)

Think beyond flowers. You're not locked into using flowers as decorations. Silk leaves, especially for an autumn wedding, add rich color. Strings of faux pearls purchased from a crafts store can be turned into swags, bows, or wreaths. Balloons are a festive, low-cost alternative, as are candles. Visit a party supply store or crafts store and you're sure to find fun flower-less ideas.

Don't Forget ...

o you feel like your brain is on overload? In the hustle-bustle of wedding planning, it's easy to overlook seemingly small, but key, details. There's been more than one frenzied couple shopping for attendant gifts the day before the wedding, or begging a limo service to spare an hour to get them from the wedding to the reception. And, yes, there's probably even a red-faced couple or two who forgot about the marriage license until the last minute.

You don't have to be one of them. Keep a notepad by your bed to jot down things that pop into your head at 2 a.m. The following four areas will get you thinking about some of the finer points that are worth tying a string around your finger.

The Rehearsal

When you're busy taking care of the zillion details of the reception and so forth, it's easy to lose sight of the rehearsal and rehearsal dinner. This warmup is usually done the night before the ceremony at the ceremony site, so you'll need to make sure the venue is available. If not, the vendor may be able to let you sneak in for a bit a few days before the wedding. Of course you'll need to make sure your attendants, officiant, and other key people can make it. When selecting the officiant, make sure you discuss the rehearsal. Some rehearsals are hour-long ordeals with the couple and attendants practicing every move and learning every cue; others are just a quick goings-over of the order.

The best part is what happens after the rehearsal: the dinner. Traditionally the groom's parents host the dinner; as discussed in Chapter 1, the conventional guidelines have changed so much that you need to clarify early on who pays for what. The main thing is to keep the dinner casual; it should be a laid-back time with your inner circle of family and friends. In a nutshell, the rehearsal dinner should help put you at ease, not be a stress-inducing event (conversely, though, it's not a repeat version of a bachelor/bachelorette party). You can reserve tables or a room in a favorite restaurant (even a pizza parlor is acceptable), or the parents may want to invite everyone over for burgers on the grill. The important thing is the camaraderie; it's a chance for the bride and groom to say thanks before the crazy day ahead.

Depending on where you want the dinner, plan to reserve the venue one to three months before the wedding. Informal invitations—even phone calls— are suitable for the pertinent parties, such as family members, attendants, readers, the officiant, and musicians (if possible). Include spouses or significant others in the invitation.

Wedding Party Gifts

When you're out and about, keep a watchful eye on possible gifts for the wedding party, parents, and other helpers. These little thank-yous are a tradition you shouldn't mess with.

That doesn't mean, however, that you have to give a done-to-death gift. A fake diamond necklace for the bridesmaids will probably be worn on the wedding day, never to be seen again until little Sally is playing dress-up. Think function when choosing gifts. Is the item something you yourself would want, need, or use? Consider each individual's tastes and interests too.

It's up to you to put a price tag on the goods and who gets them. You know who's special and who went out of his or her way to help, so you can set your own cut-off point. If you shop the right stores (outlet stores are a great place to get designer items without paying full price), you'll find great gifts for less than $50. For people who play minor roles, a $10 or $25 gift will suffice.

Consider these ideas, most of which both men and women will appreciate:

- Bathrobe
- Bottle of wine from a private winery
- Box of chocolates
- Certificate for a massage or manicure
- Certificate to a favorite restaurant
- Charitable donation in the recipient's name
- Framed photo of you and the recipient (great for any single person who may be feeling a tinge of jealousy that his or her best friend is getting married)
- Leather clutch or wallet
- Monogrammed luggage tag

Transportation

Imagine stepping out of the church, expecting to climb into a horse-drawn carriage, but seeing no carriage, no horse, no nothing. Unless you want to hoof it to the reception, make sure you have the transportation scheduled well in advance of when you need it.

If traveling to and from the ceremony and reception sites in style is important to you—and you've budgeted for it—hire a limo or luxury car service to chauffeur you to the site. If you've saved enough in other areas and you want to really impress guests, the horse-drawn carriage may be more your style. Or maybe you prefer to hire out a farmer for an old-fashioned hayrack ride (hire the person for a few extra hours so guests can enjoy rides during the reception too). Whether you go high-faluting or down-home, call around for rates and to check availability. Book the service as soon as you and your mate have agreed on what you want.

If the mode of transportation is no biggie, just fill up your gas tank the day before the wedding and give your vehicle a spin through an automatic car wash. Talk about splurges!

Legal Details

A beautiful ceremony in a rose garden or a reception that had guests dancing 'til dawn is all well and good. But if you forget the legal stuff, it's all for naught. The paperwork you'll encounter isn't glamorous, but it's a prerequisite for getting hitched. Put it on your shopping list so you don't let the legalities slip your mind and slip you up. If nothing else, look at it as protecting your investment. Consider these areas:

Marriage license. This all-important document shows your intention to get married; the marriage certificate, which is signed after the ceremony, makes things official in the eyes of the law. Requirements vary from state to state, so contact your county courthouse early on to see what's required, including who needs to be present when you apply. (The bride, groom, and one witness—all armed with photo identification—are often required to be present. You may be allowed to have the license mailed to you and signed in front of a notary.) Ask too what the fee is; usually it's minimal, such as $50 or less. But if you plan to get married in another country, the cost of a license can skyrocket, especially in popular tropical destinations where a license may be nearly $300. Depending on your state, you may need to take a blood test (consider it your last chance to ensure that you're not unwittingly marrying a long-lost, but close, relative, as well as to check for diseases). Some states require a brief waiting period after filing for a license (read that, no quickie wedding!). Also find out what proof of identification you'll need so you're not digging for birth certificates at the last minute. If you are divorced or if you are widowed, you will need to show the divorce decree or death certificate. Additionally find out how long the license is valid; in some states it expires after 30 days. A licensed officiant, judge, or justice of the peace will need to sign your license on your wedding day to validate the document. Check with your officiant to make sure he or she is licensed; if not, you'll need to make plans to get an official signature from someone else.

Name change. OK, so there's no store you'll visit that has names sitting on a shelf waiting for you to put one in the cart. Yet deciding on whether one of you wants to take the other's surname will affect you for the rest of your life. (And, yes, the groom can be the one who takes the bride's last name.) If you plan to keep your maiden name, you can bypass getting changes on your driver's license and so forth. But if you take your spouse-to-be's last name or go the hyphenated route with two last names, the floodgates are open. You'll need to update a plethora of documents: driver's license, car registration, mortgage and property titles, Social Security, passport, will, voter's registration, insurance, bank accounts, investments, and employee records, including retirement plans. If you're listed as a beneficiary on other people's wills or insurance plans, they'll need to update those too.

Will. Hopefully "until death due us part" won't come anytime soon. Regardless of age or health, though, a will is a commonsense document that will safeguard your assets in a worst-case scenario. If you don't have a will, your wedding is an ideal time to draw one up. Though a bit unconventional, it might even make a nice little gift you and your mate can give one another. Shop around for an attorney or other expert who can do the work for you. Trying to do your own will, say, from an online site, can be time-consuming and not legally binding if done incorrectly.

Wedding insurance. Say what? If you really want to safeguard your investment, look into taking out a wedding insurance policy. Though relatively new on the wedding scene, this insurance has become popular as the overall cost of a wedding has skyrocketed. If a hurricane wipes out the beach retreat you rented out, your photographer is a no-show, the caterer suddenly shuts its doors, or thieves steal your gifts, wedding insurance can help you recoup your losses. Like everything, you need to read the fine print so you know exactly what the policy does and doesn't cover. (For example, a jilted bride or groom typically can't put in a claim for a wedding that never happened.) As mentioned previously, you also need to know exactly what the contracts you signed with vendors cover; often a basic contract has the vendor's interests protected more so than yours. Call a few insurance agents to get an idea of costs (for around $150 you can usually get a policy that covers about $5,000 worth of having to cancel or postpone something), then determine if this added expense is worth it based on your overall budget—as well as your comfort level. Liability and property insurance is another area to consider; some venues may require you to get this. If a guest slips on the rose petals you sprinkled on the floor and breaks his or her wrist, or the wedding party breaks the venue's tables when they dance on them, this type of insurance will help bail you out.

eleAt

Dressing for wedding-day success

tine

doesn't need to cost a fortune!

chapter 4

No surprise here: Choosing what to wear on the big day is the bride's domain. Perhaps it dates back to dress-up days, when wide-eyed girls donned adult-size dresses, slipped on Mom's high heels, and grabbed a few flowers from a vase. Guys? Few, if any, would recall daydreaming about tails and cummerbunds.

So, gals, this is one area where you can pretty much have it your way. If your groom-to-be seems to be feigning interest as you gab about dresses, chalk it up to testosterone—and the age-old thinking that the groom should be kept in the dark about what the bride is wearing until his first glimpse of her coming down the aisle. Note to guys: Just because the bride's attire sets the tone of the wedding, it doesn't mean you don't have a say in what you wear. You don't have to don a pink bow tie and pocket square to match the bridesmaid's dresses, if that's not your idea of fashion-savvy. (Skip to "Guy Stuff," page 140.)

Of course there are brides who find the girly stuff and certain traditions to be as exciting as summer reruns. If you're one of them, by all means bend the rules. A pouffy-like-meringue gown is far from your only option. Needless to say, if you're hiking up a mountaintop to declare your love, a dress would look silly anyway. And if you loathe white, why wear it?

What you choose to wear is a way to express your individuality. Today's brides are taking an almost-anything-goes approach to real-life dress-up (or dress-down, as the case may be). Granted, a long white gown continues to top the list, but flip through bridal magazines and you'll see dresses in blush, pale golden yellow, and even with black floral overlays. Cocktail dresses, flowy cotton sundresses, and denim are on the to-wear list for some dare-to-be-different brides.

When it comes to wedding wear, the times they are a-changing. The good news—make that really good news—is that a big selection of classy and easy-on-the-budget bridal attire awaits, and there are ways to find it beyond traditional bridal salons.

Dress Dos and Don'ts

The phrase "being comfortable in your own skin" applies to wedding garb. The first rule is twofold: Find something you like and something that you're comfortable in. If you decide that's boot-scooting denim or a sequined cocktail dress, you've earned your right to it. If you're a sweats-and-T-shirt gal who thinks spending the big day in a body-hugging mermaid-style gown would be a good idea, try one. Then walk around the store and envision having the confining dress on for 12 hours. The frown on your face should be enough to convince you to find something more suitable for you.

Choosing what to wear isn't a free-for-all, though. To avoid seeming tacky or disrespectful, factor in the location and overall feel of your wedding. "The bride sets the tone of the wedding," wedding planner Jackson Lowell says. "If it's a big cathedral wedding, she can't wear a slip dress." Conversely, a fluffy Cinderella gown would be inappropriate on a sandy beach. If you did things right, you chose the site because it said something about your personalities or the desired ambiance of your shindig, so limiting your search for a site-appropriate dress or outfit shouldn't come as a surprise. In fact, it might even remove some of the burden.

To help determine what to look for, consider these general questions:

What's in your closet? The things you wear on a day-to-day basis can yield clues to what you'll feel most comfortable in on your wedding day. Is your closet filled with dresses and pumps or sweats and tennies? What do you wear to work? When you go out on the town, do you slip into a halter top and mini skirt, or do you pull out a pair of jeans from the clothes hamper? If you haven't put on a dress in years and your wedding is an informal one, a billowy wide-leg pantsuit may be your answer.

What will you be doing? If you'll be boogying 'til dawn, choose an outfit that enables you to do so without worry of splitting a seam, tripping on a train,

(continued on page 130)

Gown Glossary

From necklines to hemlines, here are some terms to know about dresses.

Dress Styles

A-line: Fitted overall with a slightly flaring skirt, creating the look of a capital A.

Ball gown: Classic Cinderella look. Fitted bodice and waist flows into a full skirt.

Basque: Fitted bodice forms a V in front, just below the waist, then usually flares into a full skirt.

Empire: Gathered just under the bust (think "high waist"), then dress falls into an A-line shape.

Mermaid: Hugs the bodice, hips, and thighs, then flares out around the knees, creating a look similar to the fictional sea creature.

Princess: Seams and darts create a flattering hourglass shape; seams may start at the bust and continue down the skirt.

Sheath: Slim and fitted, following the contours of the body, for a tailored look.

Necklines and Sleeves

Strapless: No straps or sleeves.

Sweetheart: Similar to the top of a heart-shape drawing.

Spaghetti straps: Superthin fabric straps attached to the bodice.

Off-the-shoulder: Neckline and sleeves rest below the shoulders.

Portrait: Wide scoop neck that runs from shoulder to shoulder; sleeves cover part of the upper arms.

V-neck: Deep V shape.

Halter: Straps attached to dress wrap around neck, creating a backless bodice.

Scoop neck: Deep U shape.

Cap sleeves: Just cover the shoulders.

T-shirt sleeves: End about halfway between shoulder and elbow.

Three-quarter sleeves: End about halfway between the elbow and wrist.

Long sleeves: Cover full arm, all the way to the wrist.

or showing too much cleavage. If only an hour-long cake reception follows the ceremony, you'll have a bit more leeway with tight-fitting or hard-to-move-in garments. When you try on dresses or other outfits, stand, sit, squat—basically go through the motions you'll go through on your wedding day. If having two outfits—one for the ceremony and one for the reception—is on your priority list and factored into your budget, go through the motions for each.

What's your body type? All eyes will be on you, so accentuate the positive. Choose a dress or outfit that plays up your best features—toned arms or killer legs—and hides your flaws. Knowing that people will be gawking at you can make even the most confident bride a bit self-conscious.

What's your style? You may think that having a distinct style is reserved for a select few rich and famous people. Not so. Even average folks have their own style. Tear out pages with outfits you like in catalogs and bridal magazines. Do you notice a trend? Perhaps you've selected photos of halter-style dresses or ones with A-line skirts. (See page 128 for a listing of common dress, bodice, and sleeve styles.) You're on your way to defining your personal style.

Expert Advice **Don't be afraid to ask for a discount on the dress of your dreams. "Be polite and explain to whomever you're dealing with that you absolutely adore their dress, but no way in the world will it fit in your budget," wedding planner Erika Shay says. "Tell them what you like about it and why it's the perfect dress. Usually they're going to empathize with you, and they'll want you to have the dress as well."**

When is your wedding? If you live in Alaska and want a halter-style dress for your January wedding, one thought comes to mind: Brrr! Though it's acceptable today to wear whatever you want—even a skin-baring dress in a subzero climate—it's no fun shivering or sweating through the ordeal. Factor in the time of day too. Generally morning weddings are less formal than daytime ones, and daytime weddings are less formal than evening ones.

Finding the Dress

The traditional route to getting a dress goes something like this: Bride goes to bridal salon. Bride tries on countless dresses. Bride falls in love with dress. Bride orders dress. Bride waits for dress (and waits and waits).

In years past bridal salons had a captive audience in blushing brides, most of whom had the luxury of a year to plan their weddings. Then along came the Internet, rental stores, and a whole new mindset more suited for our "I want it and I want it now" society. For now we'll stick with tradition. (The following section, "Beyond the Bridal Salon," explores alternatives.)

A bridal salon has the advantage of offering a wide selection of gowns, as well as bridesmaids' dresses, under one roof. A downside is that it can take several months (as little as two but as many as six) for the dress to be in your hands. That's all well and good if time is on your side. If not, you may need to buy off-the-rack or take another route.

To make your visit to a bridal boutique an enjoyable one, consider these tips:

Schedule an appointment. Most bridal salons require you to schedule an appointment, so call ahead to find out. There's been more than one red-faced bride with crew in tow who has stepped into a salon only to be turned away.

Bring your own fashion consultant. Most brides need, and want, a second opinion. Many use the dress shopping as a bonding experience between the mother and mother-in-law, though that can backfire. Avoid bringing all the bridesmaids, and limit your guest list to one or two people whose opinions you value and who also have an understanding of your budget.

Ask for deals. A sales clerk may not automatically steer you to the bargains, so ask for the cheap seats, so to speak, up front. Some salons will let you purchase a dress off the rack at a discount, comparable to a furniture store selling a floor model. Ask about "sample sales," when dresses that brides before you have tried on are discounted. (Check them out closely to ensure they're in good shape, or at least can be cleaned if there are makeup smudges or scuff marks on them.) Also ask if the store has a clearance or discontinued rack, or perhaps even a few dresses in the back room if a bride was a no-show. Don't be afraid to negotiate a discount for a dress you plan to order. Ask if there's a discount if you order multiple dresses—say for the bridesmaids and the mothers of the couple—from the store.

Ask the Bridal Salon

Find out the answers to these questions before you decide to do business with a bridal salon.

- How long have you been in business?

- **Is there a deposit? How much?**

- What is included in the price of the dress? Are fittings included? How many?

- **Do you charge extra for alterations? How much?**

- If I decide on a dress, when will you actually order it?

- **When will my dress arrive after you order it? Does this particular design firm or manufacturer who makes my dress meet deadlines?**

- How soon after my dress arrives can I come in for a fitting?

- **Can I cancel the order if needed? Is there a cutoff date for cancellations? Am I charged anything for a cancellation?**

- Do you have a contract I can sign?

- **Can you give me the names of some recent clients?**

Play it safe. Once you find the dress of your dreams, you may be tempted to sign on the dotted line or plunk down a deposit. Don't do it until the salon has answered key questions (see "Ask the Bridal Salon" **opposite**), and you've had a chance to call the Better Business Bureau to see if any complaints have been filed against the store. Most everyone has heard news accounts of bridal stores gone bankrupt and brides left dressless, or dresses that arrived too late for the nuptials. Some salons play Russian roulette by waiting to place orders until the last minute as a way to gain interest on deposits in the interim. Others may offer a great price on a dress but charge excessively for alterations and fittings. Ask the salon if it will hold your dress for a day or two until you have your questions answered. Some will; some won't.

Beyond the Bridal Salon

So Vera Wang didn't pan out to be your long-lost sister after all, and you don't have a thousands-of-dollars dowry earmarked for your dress. Or maybe you just can't face stepping into a store and slipping in and out of way too many dresses with way too many eyes expecting you to strut about like you're on the catwalk. Join the club. The good news is that you can get a great dress—really, truly, honestly—without secretly hocking your engagement ring or being expected to smile about all the pageantry.

Smart brides (and we bet grooms too) consider the alternatives and use their moxie to get what they want for less and usually without the wait. Consider these options for bridal gowns, bridesmaids' dresses, and even for the guys' attire:

Shop in cyberspace. Looking for dresses online can be a real timesaver. The "stores" are always open, so you can search whenever your schedule permits. It's also a great way to see what's out there and have access to things you may not find in a local store. The biggest drawback is obvious: You can't try on what you're interested in, and you won't really know what the color looks like and the fabric feels like until you get it. "If you don't allot or have enough time for the 'mistakes,' you'll be in trouble," wedding planner Angie Bloom Hewett says. If you do decide to order online, it helps to know a bit about fabric or have samples on hand so you don't end up with a supershiny fabric when you wanted something more plush. Pay close attention to the sizing charts; some may be for international sizes, so you'll need to do the math to convert (most sites will have a reference chart so you can order the proper size). It's best to stick with a style that has elements you know always look good on you, such as an Empire waist. Even better is if you've tried on the exact dress in a local store but found it cheaper on the Internet. Online prices, though, aren't necessarily cheaper, and with postage and handling included they may even cost more. You can snag some great bargains, though, at online auction sites. As with everything, read the fine print: Find out what the cancellation and return policies are, how long delivery will take, and so forth. You may be surprised to find that you have little recourse for anything—even a dress that arrives the day after the wedding.

Buy used. Oh, the thought of it ... wearing someone else's wedding gown? You bet! More and more brides have gotten over their sentimental attachment to their wedding dresses and decided it's foolish to let them be stashed away in boxes for decades. And more and more brides-to-be are scoring great deals at consignment stores and through newspaper advertisements. Pay attention and you'll find new dresses from weddings that never happened. When buying used, factor in the cost of getting the dress dry-cleaned into the overall cost. That alone can make a used dress seem brand-new, but it can also cost a hundred bucks or more to have the dress cleaned and pressed.

Rent it. There are places that rent tuxes, places that rent artwork, and places that rent yard tools. The fact that there are now places that rent bridal gowns raises the question, "Why didn't someone think of that before?" Check your phone book or ask around for stores that rent dresses. Another option is to check with a local theater company; it may be willing to rent out clothing it uses for productions. Dresses from a Shakespearean play might be just the thing to pull together a medieval-theme wedding. If the latest production was Cinderella and you're planning a princess-style wedding, you might be in luck.

Be a bridesmaid. Labels can be so deceiving. If a dress is considered a bridesmaid dress, few brides even give it a second glance. Big mistake. Many bridesmaids' dresses can step it up a notch to become your wedding gown. Bridesmaids' dresses come in white, ivory, and a plethora of other colors that are suitable for a bride—and they cost a fraction of what most wedding gowns cost.

Borrow from someone. Swallow your pride on this one. If someone you know has a dress you've long admired, muster up the courage to ask if you can wear it. She may be startled by the question but will likely be flattered. If you're asking someone you're not especially close to, such as a coworker, offer up some money as a rental fee. A caveat about borrowing: If you're inviting the same group of people who attended the dress owner's wedding, it may seem odd to see you enter in the same dress. Don't forget the bridal dress your mother, grandmother, or aunt wore. An immediate family member would likely be open to you making alterations to give the dress a more in-the-moment look.

Start plain, end fancy. Remember that underneath all the pearls and satin trims on the pricey gown you're eyeing lies a dress. Just a dress. So why not start plain and build on? Look for a plain dress, be it one at a department store or one at a bridal salon, with a style suited to your body type and a comfortable fit. Stitch on some trims and you'll have a custom gown minus the custom prices. Depending on your sewing and visualization skills, you may need to spend some money to hire a seamstress. Still, the money you saved in choosing an unembellished dress may be worth it.

Sew it up. Having a professional design and sew your wedding dress can be expensive—real expensive. But if you have a friend or relative who's handy with a needle, thread, and machine, ask him or her to do the honor of creating your dress. Make sure you've seen samples of the person's work before you ask. And, for everyone's sanity, choose a simple pattern.

Embrace the past. Many of Hollywood's hottest stars are walking the red carpet in vintage designer dresses. You can make a statement by looking in a vintage clothing store—but without shelling out the big bucks for a designer label. Though a vintage clothing store can be a treasure trove, the selection is usually limited, which means you may have to log many miles and put forth extra effort to check out a variety of stores in your area. Sizing standards are different too; you likely will need to go up a size or two from your normal "today's-standards" size. Try on a few dresses to get an idea of the fit, though that will vary depending on the era in which the garment was made. In the vintage vein, check friends' and relatives' attics for dresses that may be long-forgotten but back in style. "Vintage" now applies to even the '70s and '80s, so perhaps there's a prom dress from an older sister lurking in your parents' attic that's worth retrofitting.

Visit a department store. Don't turn up your nose at the formal attire in department stores. Dresses intended for a prom or a formal office party may work for your wedding. With a few nips, tucks, or embellishments, you can make many department-store dresses bridal bound.

The Extras

I t's often the little things that mean a lot, and that couldn't be truer with bridal accessories. Add a veil, for example, and there's no mistaking that this is a bride. Consider these tips for selecting the final flourishes:

Veil. It's dress first, veil second (or not at all; some brides choose to go without this sheer topper). The style of dress you choose will affect the type of veil that looks best. If you've chosen a mini dress, a veil that flows behind you on the floor will look awkward. Proper proportions come into play. A veil shouldn't wear you; you should wear it. And it shouldn't overshadow the dress. (See "Veil Styles" **opposite** for the options.) The headpiece is an area where you can skimp. Instead of buying a pricey veil, fashion your own from a satin-wrapped headband and a yard of tulle—or a simple hair comb and tulle. To cut the cost entirely, ask a friend or relative if you can borrow her veil; few guests will recognize that it once crowned someone else. And don't feel compelled to wear a veil. A small white flower tucked behind your ear or a cluster inserted into your updo may be all the decoration you need.

Jewelry. You'll save a few bucks if you take a cue from Oscar-bound stars and borrow the bling. Granted, you won't convince a jeweler to loan you million-dollar gems, but you can surely convince your Mom to let you wear the necklace she wore at her wedding or the brooch your great-grandmother gave her. Depending on the neckline of your dress, you might be able to skip the jewelry all together. If you must buy new, think simple so the jewelry doesn't draw too much attention. And you don't have to wear pearls! The groom often gives the bride a special trinket to wear on the wedding day. A sweet gesture, indeed, but in the interest of budget, discuss this in advance. The groom can always give the surprise early on.

Veil Styles

From shortest to longest, here's a look at veil styles.

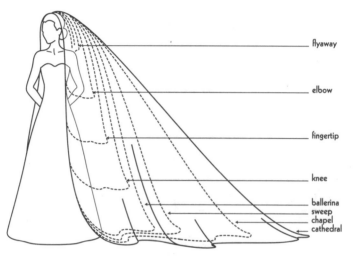

- flyaway
- elbow
- fingertip
- knee
- ballerina
- sweep
- chapel
- cathedral

Blusher

Blusher: A short veil, usually chin-length, that is worn over the face.

Flyaway: A layered portion that skims the shoulders.

Elbow: Hits between the elbow and fingertips.

Fingertip: Extends to the end of the fingertips, which is about at the hips.

Knee-length: Usually oval shape; hits at the knee.

Ballerina: Falls to about ankle-length. Sometimes called a waltz veil.

Sweep: A veil that is about 1 foot longer than where the gown ends.

Chapel: A formal veil that is about 7 feet from the headpiece.

Cathedral: Think royalty. A veil that flows behind the dress, about 12 feet from the headpiece.

Shoes. This is another area where you can skimp—at least if you're wearing a floor-length dress. No one will really be looking at your feet, and possibly no one will even be able to see them. Go for comfort. Shine up a pair that's in your closet if they complement the dress. Purchase a pair of inexpensive ballerina-style slippers. If you must have the great-looking-but-painful-to-wear pair, bring a second comfy pair for when your feet just can't take it anymore.

Gloves. Gloves are typically reserved for formal weddings, but they can also add glam to a more casual outfit. You'll probably only wear the gloves once; if money is an issue, skip them. If you must have them, look for an inexpensive pair (think crafts store or the dress-up section of a toy store).

Bridesmaids' Dresses

If you want to find out who your real friends are, ask them to be bridesmaids. Then show them a big-bowed taffeta number from a wedding you were once in, and tell them you're thinking of something like this for your own. If they don't run, it's a good sign you've chosen attendants who will be with you through thick and thin.

Measure Once ...

Getting accurate measurements for formalwear is crucial for a great fit—which is especially important for wedding-day attire that you and your attendants will be in for hours. Have a professional, such as an associate at a bridal salon or rental shop or a professional seamstress, take your measurements and use the handy chart on page 207 to record all your measurements as well as those of your attendants. This will make shopping for all your attire needs—whether in the store or online—faster and easier.

That said, you do have some responsibility to keep your bridal party happy. Instead of playing the dictator and mandating what they're going to wear, ask for their input. You'll likely hear ideas you wouldn't have thought of. Be considerate of each person's budget (the unwritten rule is that bridesmaids pay for their dresses or at least part of them) and of different body shapes.

The trend of mixing different styles of dresses has probably saved a number of friendships. You can choose the fabric, give it to bridesmaids, and tell them to make whatever they want out of it. Or just tell them to go out and find something in green. Give them each a paint chip with the shade of green you're thinking, unless you're fine with one person showing up in chartreuse and another in sage. Maybe the elusive attire is already hanging in the attendant's closet in the form of a favorite suit or cocktail dress. Leaving open the option of attendants wearing something they already own may give them much-needed financial relief—or just the relief of not having to spend days shopping for something.

The anything-goes, easy-does-it approach will earn you kudos with the attendants, as well as with guests who find it fun to see what the next ensemble marching down the aisle will be. If you go the matchy-matchy route, the same tips you followed for selecting your own dress apply. Also keep the following in mind:

Put yourself in their shoes. Would you wear the dress? Would you feel comfortable walking down an aisle or dancing in the dress? If you can answer yes to these questions, you should feel confident in presenting the choices to your attendants. A "no" answer means it's time to go back to the drawing board.

Don't exaggerate. For the sake of making bridesmaids feel at ease with the money they'll be plunking down, don't announce that the dress is something they'll be able to wear again—unless it really is something they can wear again. More than one bridesmaid has heard this but has then been presented a royal blue satin and lace number she would never be caught in at an office party. If you really want your attendants to be able to wear the outfit again, let them shop for a simple and classic cocktail-style dress or pant suit.

Don't dwell. Skipping the extras, such as shoes dyed to match the dress, gloves, and headpieces, is a goodwill gesture bridesmaids will remember. Who, after all, would ever have a need to wear satin lavender shoes again? Just ask the attendants to wear black shoes, or another basic color, and don't fret about them not being exact replicas. And guests will never know that there were matching gloves or headpieces that went with the dresses. There's no reason to expect bridesmaids to pay for all these extras that have a one-time use.

Guy Stuff

t's time for the groom-to-be to get back into the picture. Though pulling together the guy's attire is usually a breeze compared to what the bride goes through, there are some things to consider. As previously mentioned, the type of wedding affects what to wear. A nicely tailored dark suit can work for weddings that are on the informal to semiformal side. A pocket square matched to the bridesmaids' dresses adds haberdashery without much cost. If the wedding is on the shores of a lake, khakis and sandals are acceptable.

The most common route for dressing the groom and groomsmen is to rent tuxes from a formalwear shop. Renting is easy, cheap—at least compared to what brides typically encounter—and pretty much foolproof. Most brides will want to

Ask the Formalwear Shop

There are many formalwear shops listed in the phone book, but don't assume they'll have what you want when you want it. Shop around, and let the answers to these questions determine which is worthy of your business.

• What do you charge? What does the package include?

• What's your specialty? Do most of your clients rent your tuxes for weddings? Proms?

• Do you offer a quantity discount? If so, what is it?

• Do you deliver? Is there a delivery fee? If you don't deliver, when can the tuxes be picked up?

• When do the tuxes need to be returned? Is there an extra charge if they're not returned on time?

• If an item, such as a shirt or shoes, doesn't fit properly, do you have extras on hand for last-minute emergencies?

• What charges are there if a tux is returned to you soiled, torn, or otherwise damaged?

• What hours are you open? Is there a way to pick up or drop off the tuxes beyond your normal business hours?

• Is a deposit required?

make an initial visit to the formalwear shop with the groom to check out the styles. Bring along a fabric sample from the dress and the bridesmaids' dresses because not all blacks and grays are created equal.

So, guys, if tuxes are a go, consider these tips:

Shop around. Prices can vary greatly, so call around to get a general idea of costs. Find out what the store specializes in. Shops that cater to high schoolers may offer lower prices and usually a lower quality—which is fine, considering guests will never know the tux just returned from prom and they won't be inspecting the fabric's weave. Visit at least two shops so you can compare the selection and prices. (continued on page 144)

Tuxedo Talk

**Getting well-groomed applies to vocabulary too.
Learn the lingo so you can talk tails and lapels.**

Jackets, Coats, and Lapels

Cutaway: A more sculpted version of the tailcoat (see below). The waist-length front tapers into a wide tail in the back. Solid-color coat is usually teamed with striped trousers.

Double-breasted: Buttons off-center; can be a two-button or four-button front, with the buttons horizontally and/or vertically aligned.

Notched lapel: The lapel and collar join in a V shape (a slight notch). This is the most common lapel type and is less formal than the peaked lapel.

Peaked: V-shape lapel that points toward the shoulder, just below the collar line.

Shawl: A rounded lapel.

Single-breasted: Buttons in the center; can be a one- to four-button front, with the buttons vertically aligned.

Tailcoat: The utmost in formality (and bearer of penguin jokes). One or two fabric tails extend from the back waist.

Three-quarters: The length of this jacket falls about mid-thigh.

Collars

Mandarin: A stand-up collar; no "wings" or points. Can be on a shirt or jacket. Cannot be worn with a tie.

Point: A more formal version of a standard shirt collar; also called a turndown.

Spread: Resembles the point collar but is more contoured.

Wing: Formal stand-up shirt collar with points that turn down.

Accessories

  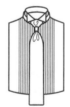 

Ascot: Wide scarflike tie fastened with a tie tack or stickpin. Fabric is usually patterned.

Bow tie: Standard bow-shape tie; can be worn with any collar style.

Euro tie: Long, square-bottom tie, often with thin stripes. A cross between an ascot and regular necktie.

Formal tie: Standard necktie, usually in silk. Smaller than a Euro tie.

Cummerbund: Horizontally pleated sash that covers the waistline of the pants. It's usually the same color as the tie and is often made of silk or satin.

Vest: A sleeveless garment, sometimes backless, worn over the shirt and under the jacket. It takes the place of a cummerbund.

Waistcoat: A more formal vest that is usually cut lower in the front.

Renting versus buying. In most cases renting is a better option than buying. But if your job or lifestyle requires you to attend black-tie affairs, go ahead and purchase a classic-style black tux. Some quality black suits can also be dressed up with a tuxedo shirt and bow tie, and no one will even know it's not a tux. A rule of thumb is that if you'll need to rent a tux two or three times a year, it's usually more cost-effective to buy one. If your weight tends to fluctuate, though, that rule may not be in your best financial interest. The last thing you want is to pay rental fees while your too-tight tux gathers dust in the closet.

Measure up. Wrapping a tape measure around your waist and jotting down a number sounds so elementary—until you get the pants to your tux on and pop a button. Being off an inch here and there on measurements is enough to cause your wedding day to be one of discomfort. Proper measurements are key to a good fit, so let the pros do it. If distance prevents the groom or a groomsman from getting to the store you're renting the garments from, it's worth it to find another method, such as asking someone in his area who does alterations to take the measurements to make sure they're done properly.

The little things. There's nothing tackier than navy socks peeking out between black pants and black shoes. Invest in a pair of socks (buy a bargain six-pack so the wedding party will have the right socks too) after you order the tux. This little detail can easily slip the mind until it's too late. If you need cuff links, make sure you have a nice set on hand.

One final note: When you get the tux, don't just throw it in the closet. Unzip the bag and check to make sure everything you ordered is in it, including the tie and pocket square. Try on the shoes. If they don't fit, you might be able to round up a different pair from the formalwear shop, or maybe swap with another member of the wedding party. You'll be happier in the long run if you take a few minutes the day before the wedding to take inventory—and your bride will have peace of mind. Time permitting, try on everything before you leave the store so you don't have to waste time on a return trip.

Other Attire Considerations

Fortunately the bulk of your work is done after the bridal dresses and tuxes are selected. The remaining details are usually painless. In fact, if you really want to take it easy, don't put any restrictions on what secondary players in your wedding wear. Of course, you'll want to let them know what you and your attendants are wearing so they don't show up in floor-length dresses or tuxes if you're all wearing shorts.

Flower girls and ring bearers. If you're having pint-size attendants, you have a lot of leeway in what they wear. A flower girl would look lovely in any white dress (dress it up with satin ribbons in your wedding colors) or a solid-color dress that complements your wedding colors. Similarly, a ring bearer can be dressed up (think suit or tux) or dressed down (black shorts and a crisp white shirt). If you want him to wear a tux, ask the formalwear shop early on if it can order a child-size one.

Ushers. Male ushers typically rent tuxes along with the wedding party, though theirs may be scaled back a bit—say, no tails. There's no rule, though, that says ushers have to wear tuxes. Dark suits are fine; don't worry about them matching. Female ushers can wear a dark-color dress or pant suit and look appropriate for the job. Some female ushers have even donned tuxedos.

Parents. Typically the fathers (or at least the father of the bride) wear tuxes. Mothers can choose what they like, be it a street-length dress, a knee-length dress, or a pantsuit. Give them key details, such as colors and photos of your attendants' dresses, so they don't end up buying something that's a near replica or that outshines what they're wearing. Stepparents should be in-the-know about the attire too.

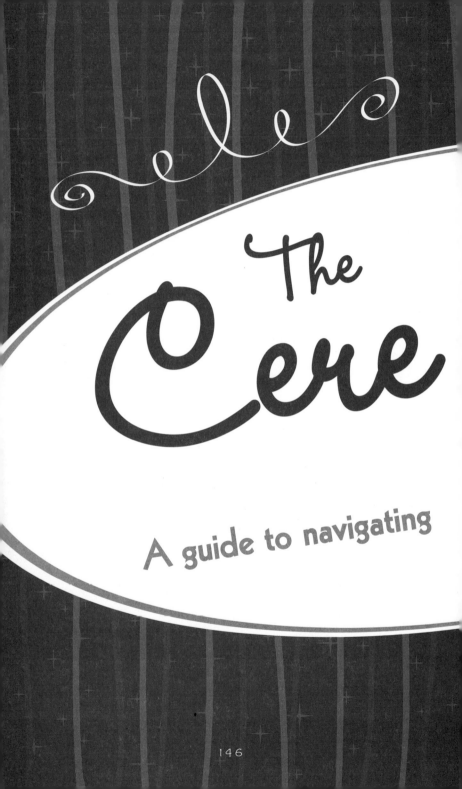

The

Cere

A guide to navigating

mony

the ceremony with ease.

chapter
5

You've probably heard horror stories of brides and grooms who fainted at the altar, downpours that drenched guests at outdoor ceremonies, or rings that were suddenly MIA. Relax. If a worst-case scenario happens during your wedding, there's really not much you can do about it, other than to smile (well, at least try to) and let the show go on. Every wedding—from finely honed formal affairs to casual-as-can-be ceremonies—has a few glitches, albeit some bigger than others, but most are worth a laugh down the road.

Wouldn't it be nice if you could gaze into a crystal ball to see where your ceremony would go astray, and right the wrongs before the big day arrived? Well we foresee this: There are no crystal balls in your future. Even though you can't control the weather or tame a bad case of nerves, proper planning can ward off evil spirits in other areas, the most notable of which is letting the budget get out of control.

Refresher Course

The No. 1 rule for making it through the wedding day is to clear your schedule. No matter how big a hand you've had in planning the wedding or how much of a DIY couple you are, it's time to let things go. No bride or groom wants to be in the kitchen whipping up batches of buttercream frosting hours before they're walking down the aisle.

The best thing you can do is agree to hand over the reigns to a trusted friend or a wedding planner. (Remember you can hire a coordinator for just the day's events. Refer back to the wedding planner section in Chapter 1.) "If you're the type who needs everything to happen at a certain time, it's definitely worth it to hire a planner to work the day of the wedding," says wedding planner Matt O'Dorisio. If you haven't budgeted for this one-day luxury, you'll need to think through all the little details and write them down to make sure everyone knows where they're expected to be and when. (See "Ceremony Itinerary" on page 160 for more information; see also "Reception Timeline" in Chapter 6, page 186, for information about setting a timeline after the ceremony.)

By the time you're reading this, you should have already booked the location of your ceremony. If not, refer to Chapter 2, which covers shopping around for a venue. If so, it's still worth a look back at that section to see if there are things you forgot to ask. A few things of which to be especially mindful:

Name that tune. Make sure you know what type of music the site allows or prohibits. Some churches, for example, only allow very traditional songs; you may need to pass your selections by the officiant or choral leader for approval. Logistics may play a part in the music too. If you're getting married on the beach, you're probably not planning to lug an organ to the sandy shore. For more on music, see "Personalize It" on page 155.

Decked out. Decorations are another area that needs clarification. Are you allowed to bring in your own decorations, and are there any restrictions on what you can do (no nail holes, nothing on an altar, and so forth)? When can you get in to decorate, and when must you have them removed? Perhaps you chose the site or the specific day because the decorations would already be in place.

Decorating Dos

If you'll be decorating your ceremony site, consider these tips for keeping the budget in line.

• Put your money in what will be seen most: the altar or other area where you are standing.

• Use in-season flowers to avoid extra costs.

• Consider the logistics and time frame. If you're doing the decorating and you can't get into the venue until an hour before the wedding, you won't have time to do much.

• Skip the bows on pews or seats. Or place them only on every other row or every fifth row.

• Choose flowers with big blooms, such as hydrangeas, mums, or peonies. It will take fewer flowers to make an impact.

• Check into rentals—for potted plants, arches, bouquets, and candelabras—from florists, large crafts stores, and rental shops.

• See if you can use any decorations the site has on hand. A church, for example, might welcome you volunteering to put up holiday decorations a week earlier than planned. Even being able to use vases, candlesticks, an aisle runner, or candelabras will save some money. Similarly, if there's another event happening at the site the same day— even another wedding—you might be able to tag-team on decorations. Don't be afraid to ask.

Better check on that too. The pumpkins and mums you envisioned being in place for your November wedding at the rustic lodge may be removed after the annual October Fall Fest. The poinsettias and Christmas tree may not go up in the church until the day after your wedding. If you counted on those "freebies" as a way to keep your budget in line, you'll need to get extra creative. Keep in mind that a ceremony may last anywhere from just 10 minutes to an hour, so you'll need to use some additional creativity to get your money's worth out of the decorations, and ideally use them for both the ceremony and the reception. Making your own decorations or finding creative new uses for ordinary items is not only cost-effective, but they can be the ooh-la-la of your big day. The ceremony sites on **For Better or For Worse** have come to life by such imaginative touches as fashioning fabric-covered chicken wire into perhaps the world's largest bow to add elegance to a Wild West setting, dangling orchids from fishing line to hang above an altar, using sod to create a lush grass aisle, and turning an altar into a giant lattice "window" complete with flower-filled window boxes. (See page 225 for do-it-yourself projects, including instructions for the window frame altar.)

Hit the books. Some ceremony sites, typically churches and other religious affiliations, require premarital classes. If yours is one of them, get that on your docket. For other official considerations, see "The Officiant" **below**.

The Officiant

Depending on where you're getting hitched, you may or may not have a choice of who's leading the I dos. If the ceremony is in a church, synagogue, or other house of worship, the officiant may be assigned to you, or, if it's a larger site, you may be given a choice of whom you'd like to perform the ceremony. If you have different religions or have a relative or friend who's a member of the clergy, you may want to have two people officiate, with approval from the venue.

Ask the Officiant

If you have the option of choosing an officiant, ask these questions to make sure your marriage will be on the up-and-up and to keep the ceremony as flawless as possible. Tailor the questions as needed, depending upon whether your ceremony is religious or nonreligious in nature. Keep asking around until you're satisfied you've found the person who best suits your needs.

• Are you legally certified to perform weddings? By whom?

• Are you available on the date and time we're getting married?

• What is your fee, or what is the expected honorarium or donation?

• What requirements or restrictions do you have regarding the formality of the ceremony, choice of vows, and selection in music, decorations, photography, attire, end-of-ceremony sendoffs such as throwing birdseed, and other things?

• Do you have any restrictions regarding interfaith marriages? Divorces? Second (or whatever number applies) marriages?

• Are we required to take any premarital classes? If so, when, for how long, and how many?

• If we want certain people to take part in the ceremony, such as reading a selection, is that possible? Do you allow a co-officiant? If so, can the person be from another religion?

• How long do your ceremonies typically last? Can we cut out or add parts if desired?

• Can we form a receiving line at the site if desired?

• What restrictions, if any, do you have on photography and videography during the ceremony?

• What requirements do you have for signing the marriage certificate? How soon will you sign and send the certificate to the proper authority?

• Are you performing any other ceremonies the day of our wedding, and are there any potential time conflicts?

• Do you require a rehearsal? Are you available for it?

• How soon before the wedding will you arrive?

• Can we have someone chime the bells if desired?

• Do you attend the reception and offer a blessing before the food is served if desired?

If the ceremony isn't in a church and you're not headed to an all-hours chapel, you'll need to shop around for an officiant. A good starting point is a religious leader—a priest, minister, or rabbi, for example. Even if you're not getting married at the person's house of worship, he or she may be willing to perform the ceremony. Some, though, may consider it only if it's a religious ceremony. Be up-front about what you have planned as well as your personal convictions so the person you contact can make an informed decision as to whether he or she is the right person for the job or even feels comfortable doing it. The fact that you've been living together for a year, the bride is pregnant, this is your third marriage, or you're from different religions may not bother you, but a religious officiant could have objections or conflicts with performing the ceremony. It's better to get things out in the open than to have the officiant back out at the last minute.

If you're planning a nonreligious ceremony, you can look for an officiant in the ranks of a county courthouse (judges, magistrates, and clerks are typically authorized), a city's mayoral office, a roadside chapel, or a friend who's newly ordained via the Internet. Make sure you know the laws in the state and/or country in which you're getting married so you know the person, and subsequently your marriage, is legit. Call a county courthouse, mayor's office, or other authority to find out who's licensed or can be licensed to perform weddings in your state.

The Marriage License

Forget the rings, the vows, the tender moments. The little piece of paper that seals the deal is the most important thing on your wedding day—not that most people will even see it. We covered much of what you need to know in Chapter 3, but it's worth repeating here. The first step is to get a marriage license. This is basically nothing more than an intent to get married. You both need to sign the license, and usually one or two witnesses will need to be present when you apply for it, though this varies depending upon your state. After the actual ceremony, the bride, groom, officiant—a person legally certified to conduct weddings—and a witness or two must sign an actual marriage certificate, which declares that you followed through on your intent to get married. Usually the bride and groom leave the certificate with the officiant to complete and mail to the issuing authority.

Find out how your officiant wants to make the signatures happen. Usually it's just a quick, informal procedure after the ceremony—nothing fancy, and no one watching except the witness or witnesses. The officiant will need to get the marriage certificate returned to the appropriate authority within the predesignated time frame, such as 90 days. After that you will receive a certified copy of the marriage certificate. To avoid missing deadlines and having a crisis on your hands, it's critical that you know the expiration dates and time frame for getting things filed; these vary among states and countries. Another word of warning: Check the expiration date when you apply for the license; if you've applied too early, the license may no longer be valid by the time your wedding rolls around. In some states marriage licenses are valid only for 30 days.

It's a whole new ballgame if you're getting hitched in another country. Make sure you know the laws of the land; you may need to hire a wedding coordinator or other trusty someone at your destination to find out all the legalities and help you take care of them.

The Vows

Long before your wedding day arrives, you'll need to decide whether you're a "to love, honor, and obey" kind of couple. The big question: Should you go with traditional vows, write your own, or have the officiant tweak the traditional ones so they're slightly more modern?

There's no right or wrong answer; it's something you need to figure out as a couple—and, of course, working within the restrictions of your ceremony site and/or officiant. Some people think sharing personally written sentiments in front of a group is sappy or too intimate to share; others get weepy-eyed at the romanticism and poetry of it. Consider these tips (and pros and cons) for figuring out what vows you want to say:

Write away. If you plan to write your own vows, ask the officiant if that's allowed. If so, set some guidelines. Limit the vows to a predetermined number of words or time frame, say three minutes max, and start drafting your missives early. Experiencing writer's block the day before the ceremony isn't a good feeling. Don't get hung up on trying to be a poet; look at it as penning a brief message to your soul mate. Whatever you do, don't pawn off the job on someone else unless you want your first blowout as newlyweds. Set a deadline for each of you to have the vows written, say two weeks before the wedding. Set a midterm check-in deadline too. After a few drafts, you may both decide that "in sickness and in health" doesn't sound so bad after all. Find out if the officiant needs to review the vows in advance and, if so, when he or she needs them.

Oldie but goodie. If writing isn't your thing, it's best to just go with vows from the officiant so you don't have another stress heaped on your shoulders. Ask the officiant to show you the typical vows or the choices in vows. Then set aside an hour to go over the wording on your own. You can strike phrases such as "promise to obey" or others and talk over replacements with the officiant.

Tradition with a twist. Some couples who are blending families include their children in their vows. A groom, for example, may say his vows to the bride, and then turn to the bride's child to pledge his love and devotion as a stepfather. Conversely, a larger blended family may have children pledging their devotion to the parents and stepparents as a sign that the family is unified. Widowed or previously divorced brides and grooms may also want to consider twists to traditional vows. Make sure the officiant gives prior approval.

Personalize It

After talking with the officiant, you'll have a better idea of what is and isn't off-limits during your ceremony. You'll also be able to think of ways to customize your wedding to fit your personalities and situation. Consider these ideas for putting a personal touch on common ceremony elements:

Joyful refrain. Though the ceremony site and officiant will often dictate choices in music, this is an area where you can really personalize your wedding without much, if any, expense. A cousin who plays the trumpet can kick off the processional, and a choir of your best friends can chime in on vocals. When selecting music consider the site and the formality of your wedding. "Ave Maria" may be great for a formal church wedding but will seem out of place in a barn down a dirt road. A favorite tune that's on the playlist of a pop radio station may be better left to the reception dance because everyone will have that version in their minds. The site's acoustics should come into play too. A violin solo in one church will sound entirely different in another or outdoors, for example. Using friends and relatives for singing and playing music is often a preferred route because it's so personal and, well, free. If you don't have musically inclined acquaintances, though, there are other low-cost alternatives. Have guests provide the vocals, comparable to a congregation singing in church; choose simple melodies or familiar lyrics. For a $25 to $75 honorarium, you can likely get a choir member from a music department of a church, college, or high school. A flutist from a high school marching band or a violinist from a college symphony can offer a low-budget reprieve from the typical organ music. If you plan to use a stranger, require an audition, preferably at the place where your ceremony will be held. Don't overdo it on the music; three songs during the ceremony is usually plenty.

Special remembrances. If there's someone or something special to you, the ceremony can be a time to pay tribute. You can have a bouquet at the altar or place a rose in a vase in honor of a deceased parent or other special someone. If you don't have the money for an altar bouquet or more flowers, light a candle or have the person's favorite song sung or played. Special remembrances don't have to be somber. A groom on leave from the military may want a few words said about his fellow soldiers. On a more lighthearted note, if you met your mate at a Shakespearean festival, you might tap an actor to recite a few lines, or if you met while walking dogs in a park, maybe the canines are led down the aisle on leashes. The key on such special touches, especially somber ones, is not to dwell on them too long; after all, the day is supposed to be about you. If you'd rather have a more private tribute, take a few minutes before or after the ceremony to reflect on things, or make a mention in the wedding program ("We dedicate this day to the soldiers serving our country" or "The peony on the altar is in memory of the bride's mother. This was her favorite flower.").

Ceremonial send-off. Things used to be so simple with just-married couples: Guests grabbed handfuls of rice to lob at the couple as they left the ceremony site. In a politically correct environment, rice is a huge no-no; it's bad for birds who try to eat it and it's rather slippery to walk on. Try birdseed instead. Of course, the options don't end there. You can have guests toss flower petals, ring small handheld bells, or blow bubbles. Unless you're into complicating things, steer clear of living creatures. Save the white doves and butterflies for someone else. Figure out too if the logistics even enable a special send-off to happen—or if you want it. This is an area you can ax to give your budget some relief.

The Order

Here comes the bride ... and the bridesmaids and the groomsmen and the groom. But in what order? How you choose to parade out the wedding party and seat guests depends upon the ceremony site, formality of your wedding, and possible restrictions from the officiant. Certain religions call for a specific order for the processional and recessional. Casual ceremonies can stick with tradition, or someone can simply holler "Let's start" and everyone can take their place at a makeshift altar. Remember that things may vary depending upon the site and the officiant. Use the following traditional guidelines to bring order to your ceremony:

Seating. In a traditional Christian wedding, the bride's family sits on the left as you're facing the altar, and the groom's family is on the right. It's the opposite with Jewish ceremonies. As such, check with the officiant or other person in the know to ensure you don't make any seating faux pas. Other tricky situations include divorced parents. Unless there's some especially jovial relationship or prior agreement, divorced parents should be seated in separate rows (mother in front row; father in second row). Special guests can be escorted to their seats just before the processional begins. The groom can escort parents, stepparents, or grandparents to their seats, or you can designate one of the ushers to do this. This special element should be reserved only for truly honored guests; if you also make a production out of escorting siblings, aunts, uncles, and cousins, you'll diminish the importance of those very special guests.

Processional. If you're having a religious ceremony, talk to the officiant about the processional details and any restrictions. Some officiants adhere to strict or traditional guidelines regarding how the bride, groom, attendants, and parents should walk in, and these vary among denominations. The officiant, for example, may not allow the groom to escort the bride down the aisle before the ceremony—something modern couples sometimes desire. In Jewish ceremonies grandparents are usually a part of the processional. To make sure you don't leave anyone out or to avoid last-minute changes, which would require a late-night scramble to redo the wedding programs, ask the officiant about this well before the rehearsal rolls around. If you're having a nonreligious ceremony, a typical processional has the officiant, groom, and groomsmen waiting at the altar as the bridesmaids come down the aisle, ending with the bride's honor attendant. Next comes the ring bearer, followed by the flower girl; sometimes they walk down as a pair. Last, but certainly not least, is the bride, escorted by her father (or other escort) on her right side and, sometimes, the mother on the left side. Guests should stand for the bride, but stay seated for the others.

Recessional. When the ceremony is over, the newlyweds and attendants traditionally walk down the aisle in pairs, with the bride and groom leading the way. Make sure you cover the ending with the officiant so you don't start walking out before he or she has introduced you or otherwise finished.

Receiving line. After the ceremony, it's tradition for the bride and groom to greet guests. Depending upon your situation, this can be done at the ceremony site, though traditionally it's done at the reception. Like many wedding elements, the receiving line has strayed from traditional guidelines on where it should be and who should be in it (women only, aside from the groom, according to the strictest interpretation). Check with your officiant or the venue manager on any rules regarding where the line may form; your schedule may also dictate this. If you're taking all the photos after the wedding, you'll need to have the receiving line at the ceremony site because you won't be around to greet guests as they arrive at the reception. Form the line at the back of the church, vestibule, or outdoors. To keep the line moving, there's no need to have attendants be part of the receiving line. Just limit it to the bride, groom, and parents/stepparents. The bride and groom should be in the center of the line, with parents flanking them. If there are divorced parents and strained relations, mix up the order so the bride's mother stands next to the groom's father, and so forth. Some couples prefer the mixed order so there's always someone near who knows who the guest is—for example, the bride's mother can introduce the groom's father to her relatives or friends the groom's father hasn't yet met. Some couples skip the receiving line for something less formal: For example, after the wedding party has marched down the aisle after the ceremony, the couple returns to usher guests out of their seats, starting at the front row. A benefit is that there's no lengthy conversations that slow things down. A smile and simple "We're happy you're here" is enough to suffice for most guests.

Looking Good

Whether you have 100 eyes staring at you or just a handful, every bride and groom wants to look and feel their best on their wedding day. That's understandable, considering it takes a fair amount of courage and self-confidence to be the centers of attention. Add to that the fact that film and video can be unforgiving, recording every dark under-eye circle or unruly hair.

You're not being vain and superficial if you find yourself dwelling on your exterior. But if you plan to splurge on hairdos, facials, and manicures, you'll need to cut back in other areas or be creative in your interpretation of what the services entail. That said, there's no reason you have to splurge on all this. If you can't afford a professional manicure, for example, buy a fresh bottle of nail polish and give yourself one. Your nails will look better, you'll feel better—and your budget is out just a $3 bottle of polish. Set aside a "beauty night" (the groom is invited!) a few days before your wedding to pamper yourself at home. Deep-condition your hair, give and get a manicure and pedicure, give yourself a facial with a self-applied mask, and even give each other a back rub.

Whatever you do, refrain from an extreme makeover. Brides who have never worn makeup should go easy on it, just as brides who have never colored their hair should refrain from altering their color the day before the wedding. The groom's first glimpse of the bride should be followed by a smile, not a puzzled "who is that?" look. Grooms should also refrain from changes, such as shaving off the decades-old beard or wearing contact lenses if you usually wear glasses.

Here are some considerations for the beauty regime, for both the bride and the groom: (continued on page 162)

Quick Tip Attention brides and bridesmaids! If you're putting your hair in an updo on the wedding day, you can skip washing it. Sound gross? Squeaky-clean hair is more difficult for stylists to work with, and it won't hold pins as well. Wash your hair before you go to bed the night before the wedding (or no sooner than 12 hours before the ceremony), apply the usual product, and dry as usual. No one except the stylist will ever know you didn't shampoo.

Ceremony Itinerary

Make sure everyone involved in your wedding knows where to be and when. Complete this itinerary and use the information to make agendas to distribute to pertinent parties several weeks before your wedding. (Also bring extra copies to hand out on the wedding day.) Include phone/cell numbers of each person so everything is on one handy sheet if last-minute calls need to be made the day of the ceremony. For recommendations on creating a reception itinerary, see "Reception Timeline," page 186.

Bride arrives at ceremony site:_____

Bridesmaids arrive at ceremony site:_____

Groom arrives at ceremony site:_____

Groomsmen arrive at ceremony site:_____

Immediate family members arrive at ceremony site (if needed, specify who this pertains to):_____

Officiant arrives at ceremony site:_____

Florist arrives at ceremony site:_____

Ushers arrive at ceremony site:_____

Bride's personal attendant arrives at ceremony site:_____

Guest-book attendant arrives at ceremony site:_____

Photographer arrives at ceremony site:_____

Photography begins at:_____

Others:_____

_____

_____

_____

Name, address, and phone number of ceremony site:_____

_____

Your primary contact the day of ceremony:_____

Contact's cell phone number:_____

Sample Ceremony Itinerary

Ceremony Itinerary and Tasks for the wedding of John Smith and Jane Doe

Location: XYZ Community Hall, 555 5th St., Anytown, Arizona
Date: Saturday, July 23, 2005

Pre-Ceremony
10 a.m.–12:30 p.m. Hair and makeup for bride, bride's attendants, and bride and groom's mothers.
Meet at XYZ Salon, 555 7th St. Remember to wear a buttoned or zippered shirt that you won't have to pull over your head.

11 a.m.–Noon Groom and groom's attendants.
Meet at XYZ Fitness Center for light workout followed by a quick lunch.

10 a.m.–1 p.m. Decorate church, pick up floral arrangements, help musicians and photographer get situated, place guest book and wedding programs.

Amy Doe is in charge of the ceremony tasks. Her cell phone number is 555/555-5555. Others helping her are Frank Doe, Lou and Mary Johnson, and Jennifer Miller.

The contact for the church is Frances Madsen. Her phone number is 555/555-5556.

1 p.m. Bride, groom, and their family members arrive at church.
Wedding party arrives at church. (Note: Spouses and children are welcome to come at this time, if desired.)

1:30 p.m.–4 p.m. Photos.
(Note: Family group photos will be taken toward the end of the session, starting about 3:15 p.m.)

3 p.m. Ushers arrive at church.
(photos at 3:45 p.m.)
(Note: Spouses and children are welcome to come at this time, if desired).

4 p.m. Officiant arrives.
Bride and groom meet briefly with officiant.

Vocalist/musicians arrive.

Bride/bridal party wait in north conference room.

Groom/groom's party wait in south conference room.

Head usher moves couple's car to front of church.

5 p.m.–5:45 p.m. Ceremony.

5:45 p.m. Couple signs marriage certificate.
Head usher drives couple to reception, where receiving line will form.

Hair. Hair has become a big thing with many brides. It's common today for a stylist to come to the wedding site, or for the female members of the wedding party to pay a visit to a stylist hours before the ceremony.

How the bride will wear her hair should ideally be determined four to eight weeks before the wedding; a trial "run-through," with veil or headpiece in hand, is common. It's a good idea to take a photo (front, side, and back) of the style or updo you like best so your stylist has something to refer to on the big day. (Even the most on-the-ball stylist sees so many clients that it's easy to forget the details, so bring a camera to your appointment and have the stylist snap a few quick photos.) Bridesmaids don't need a run-through, but the stylist does need plenty of time to address each individual. Allot one hour per bridesmaid. Mothers may also welcome the chance to have a professional style their hair on the wedding day, so include them in the festivities. Another benefit: Stylists report that many mothers end up picking up the tab. Don't leave it to chance, though. Determine in advance who is paying for what. Many brides budget in the cost of the bridesmaids' styling; making a bridesmaid pay for yet another little extra may send the person over the edge.

Haircuts for both bride and groom should be done about four weeks before the wedding, though this varies from person to person. Highlights or coloring should be done two weeks before the wedding; if it's done any sooner, you likely will have outgrowth or roots showing.

Less glamorous to talk about is the hair sprouting from ears, noses, chins, and eyebrows. And, yes, it applies to both men and women—though men have more chance of wayward hairs. Have them taken care of the week of the wedding. Enough said.

Makeup. This is the woman's domain. If you're hiring a makeup artist, you may need to schedule a run-through, similar to a hair run-through. If hiring someone is out of your budget, make a few visits to a makeup counter at a department store, where you can usually get a makeover for free. Even if you don't purchase the products, you'll gain tips on what works and doesn't work for your skin type. Your photographer may have some tips too. Bright red lips and too much blush can leave a bride looking like a clown in photos. Go lightly; it's easier to add than to subtract. Waterproof mascara is a must, even for brides who swear they won't cry.

Skin. First, forget the deep, dark tan. It's a thing of the past, even though self-tanners make it easy to achieve a golden glow. If you've ever seen wedding photos of an overly bronze bride or groom (with gleaming white teeth, comparatively), you'd quickly realize how a tan doesn't translate well into photographs. Save the cost of self-tanners or a tanning bed.

A facial, on the other hand, can work wonders for getting your face looking and feeling its best. A facial isn't just for brides. More men are opting for facials before their wedding to clear up pores and soften their skin. Drinking a lot of water is a natural treatment, so indulge in plenty of this no-cost elixir the weeks leading up to the wedding. Schedule facials at least two weeks in advance to avoid unexpected bad reactions. Similarly, don't try new skin-care products or makeup for several weeks before the wedding.

Nails. If you're having a manicure and/or pedicure, schedule it a day or so before the wedding. If your wedding week is already overbooked, make the appointments earlier; you may need to touch up nails, but it's better to get it out of the way so you're not trying to work one in, along with details that can't be done until the last minute. If your budget is looking bleak on these little extras, skip the pedicure because the focus will be on hands and the new bling on them, not on the feet. If money is really an issue, do your own manicure, as mentioned earlier. Choose clear or a pearly polish; anything colorful is distracting. The groom should also make sure his nails are in tip-top shape, so get out the nail clipper and file.

Massage. One of the best gifts you can give one another is a his-and-her massage. Make it a deep massage and an hour-long session. Schedule it the week before the wedding if your schedule is looking too booked to get it done a few days before the event. If a massage isn't in the budget, take a slow walk around a lake or a nap curled up together on the sofa, with soft music playing in the background. The goal is relaxation and clearing your mind after all the hectic months or weeks spent planning your wedding.

Don't Forget ...

There's no reason for Murphy's Law to prevail on your wedding day. Put the following easy-to-forget and sometimes overlooked items on your to-do list. (For that matter, put making a to-do list on your list; it's a great way to gauge what you have done and what you need to accomplish before the big day arrives.)

Rings. Make sure there's a plan to pick them up from the jeweler and get them to the ceremony. Often the groom entrusts the best man (or honor attendant) with this. During the ceremony, the bride's maid/matron of honor (or honor attendant) tends to the groom's ring. Seldom is a ring bearer entrusted with the rings; that's a little too much responsibility for a little guy!

Marriage certificate. Don't leave home without it. Unless you've made prior arrangements to get the certificate to the officiant, someone will need to make a trip home to retrieve this all-important document if you show up without it. Some officiants will ask you to bring it to the rehearsal—not a bad idea to ensure it gets in the proper hands.

Ceremony itinerary. You may know exactly when the show gets under way, but others don't know when you expect them to be at the ceremony site—aside from making it by the time noted on the invitation. Instead of keeping them guessing—and making them and their families a little irritated—make an itinerary for the day's events and distribute it to attendants, family members, and key players several weeks before your wedding. This handy piece of paper isn't only a courtesy for your wedding party; it will also alleviate countless "Where do I go?" and "What time do I need to be there?" last-minute phone calls that you'll need to tend to. See "Ceremony Itinerary," page 160.

Fees and tips. As discussed in Chapter 1, you'll likely dole out a lot of money on your wedding day. Fees, gratuities, and honorariums for officiants, musicians, servers, and so forth are typically given after the event. Place the respective payment in an envelope with the person's name written on the outside. Typically the best man (or groom's honor attendant) doles out the money, so give the envelopes to that person or another preappointed person, along with some $1 and $5 bills for tips for people who go above and beyond.

Survival kit. Pack a small bag with the little things you can never seem to find when you need them most: aspirin, safety pins, a pair of black socks for the groom or groomsmen, a pair of panty hose for the bride or bridesmaids, facial tissue, small scissors, dental floss, an extra pair of contact lenses—anything you can think of that you would be very sorry if you didn't have. Don't wait until your wedding day to pack the bag because you'll be too distracted or harried to really pay attention to what needs to go in it.

Food and drink. It sounds basic, but grabbing a bite to eat and drinking plenty of water before the ceremony is a must. Ever wonder how many of those fainting brides or grooms had been too busy or distracted to eat a decent meal and drink a few glasses of water? Don't fool yourself into thinking you'll save the nourishment for the reception; many a bride and groom report that they didn't even get a chance to enjoy what they served guests. A light meal an hour or so before you head to the ceremony site may be one of the smartest things you do before getting hitched.

ele

The

Rece

Ways to eat, drink,

ption

and be merry.

chapter
6

When the reception rolls around, you're almost there—you're on the downhill slope and close to declaring victory. Your thoughts have turned to the honeymoon and, perhaps, chucking your wedding-planning binder into the nearest body of water. You probably feel like you could scale a mountain and do a happy dance on the highest summit to declare that you did it. You planned a wedding and you survived—a bit weary but unscathed.

All of the above is usually true when the reception rolls around. But you haven't reached the "when" stage yet. Between now and the time you say goodbye to the last lingering guest, there's a lot to do. The wedding ceremony? Heck, that's a cakewalk compared to planning the reception. The typical reception, after all, is an event extraordinaire that requires finite details and impeccable timing to ensure the food is warm (or cold, depending upon what you're serving), the centerpieces are pretty (and not blocking guests' views across the table), the cake is intact (and tasty), the musicians have arrived (and aren't drowning out conversations), the bar is open (and there's something for everyone), and the guests are happily mingling (and not complaining about the aforementioned atrocities).

Unlike the wedding, which is all about you, the reception is all about your guests. Your prime concern should be to make guests feel comfortable and welcome while they're there—and feel happy and satisfied when they walk out the door. Between Point A, where you are now, and Point Z, where you need to be when your wedding day rolls around, you need to put on your thinking cap to plan the party of your lifetime. Wedding planner Erika Shay notes that the average reception can eat up 70 percent of the overall budget. You need to make sure it's money well spent.

Back to the Basics

There's good news on at least one front: By now you should have already figured out the nitty-gritty of where to hold the reception, when to hold it, and the overall type of reception you want. If not, turn back to Chapters 1, 2, and 3 for ideas and the know-how to find and get a great venue.

Don't panic if you're reading this and you still haven't booked a reception site. Traditional venues, such as reception halls, hotel ballrooms, and country clubs, book up early and may be out of the picture for last-minute shoppers—unless you are fortunate to snag venues after late cancellations, which has been a cost-saving measure for the **For Better or For Worse** wedding planners more than once. But that may be a blessing in disguise. Search off the beaten path and think outside the box, and you'll discover an endless array of possibilities for a one-of-a-kind reception. A bonus: You might stumble upon a real deal, moneywise. A historical group in a small town might be eager to let you use its mansion for $25, in exchange for showing off its artifacts. An unknown artist who has just opened a tres cool gallery might be willing to give you the roam of the place to gain exposure for his or her works. A barn that doesn't seem like much of an attraction to a farmer who owns it may be just the rustic retreat you desire. It never hurts to ask.

Refer to Chapter 2 and throughout this book for creative ideas on choosing a venue. A few key points are worth repeating here:

You want it when? Ceremony first, reception second. You can't argue with that logic. Because the reception is in honor of a newly married couple, it only makes sense that it comes after the ceremony. What you can argue with is the logic of when the reception is held. It doesn't have to come immediately after the ceremony, as is traditionally done. If your heart desires—and perhaps your schedule mandates—you can hold the reception a week later, a month later, or six months later. In these cases the ceremony is usually a supersmall gathering, perhaps held at a city hall, your parent's living room, or far, far away. (If you had a full-blown ceremony, it wouldn't make sense to call in guests for that and then convene them again a week or month later for the reception.) If you have your heart set on a certain reception site, having flexibility in the reception date may enable you to get your first choice after all.

Serve up style. Similar to how many couples feel locked into having the reception right after the ceremony, they may also feel locked into a traditional sit-down meal or a filling buffet. The time of day plays a big part in what you serve and how you serve it. Some stylish alternatives to a full meal include a midafternoon cocktail party, where guests mingle around cocktail tables and munch on appetizers, and a Sunday brunch with champagne or mimosas flowing

(continued on page 172)

Reception Planning

If you're still debating what type of reception to have, your answers to these questions should offer some clues about your comfort level on formal and fancy versus casual and no-frills—as well as where you can save.

1 **The best party you've ever attended most closely resembled:**

a) enjoying a multicourse meal at a swank restaurant.
b) a dinner party at a friend's house with a spread of your favorite foods.
c) drinks and finger foods as you mingled with guests.
d) a midafternoon gathering with friends and delicious desserts.

There's no right answer, but this question should get you thinking about the attitude of the party you want to throw for your guests. Both a formal meal and a free-flowing appetizer reception are equally fun, but each creates a different feel for the celebration.

2 **True/False. Providing an array of snacks for your guests can make your food costs add up quickly.**

This is a trick question. Depending upon the food choice, it can become costly, but there are a lot of inexpensive options: bread and cheese, nuts and in-season fruit, chips and salsa, vegetables and dip. Mini quiches and tartlets are swell, but your guests will enjoy any food that you typically snack on at home as long as it's well presented.

3 **When you hit the casino for a night of fun you:**

a) take $20 for the nickel slot machines and head home when you're out of cash.
b) take the bonus you received from work and put it all on red at the roulette table.
c) plan on spending $50 to play Black Jack, but you bring your ATM card—just in case.
d) buy a drink, see a show, and head home—because the house always wins.

There's a lot of trust involved in asking someone to do a particular job for you on your big day—and trust goes hand-in-hand with risk. If you're willing to plunk your money down and let it ride, then you might be comfortable asking a friend to take your wedding pictures, hiring a student DJ you've never heard to play for the reception, or entrusting your wedding cake to a family member who's never made one before—all in the name of saving money. But if you're terrified of not knowing if you'll hit the jackpot on the slot machines, you might be better off sticking with (slightly more expensive) professionals.

4 True/False. You've kept the favor from every wedding ever attended.

Come on, false, right? For the most part, people comment on how cute the favors are and then throw them away when they get home. Your guests will do the same thing. Remind yourself of this when you're choosing what, if anything, to offer and your budget starts ballooning out of control. The trick is to create simple, personalized, and possibly edible favors that don't take a lot of time or a large chunk of change.

5 An element on your wedding day that can perform double duty is:

a) the flower arrangements.
b) the musicians.
c) the ceremony site.
d) the wedding party.

If you guessed all of the above, you're right. Flower arrangements can be moved from the ceremony to the reception, and the ceremony site can be quickly transformed to accommodate dinner and dancing— a trick the wedding planners on For Better or For Worse **often use to** stretch their budgets—and the wedding party can help with everything from seating the guests to serving the cake. The more you double up on items, the more money you save.

6 True/False. A memorable reception lasts well into the night.

False. There's no reason why your reception has to go until the break of dawn. In fact you'll rack up overage fees at your site, and your DJ won't stay to play for free! Your guests might even appreciate it if you held the wedding earlier in the afternoon, followed by a reception that ends by midafternoon. Your guests may decide to head off to dinner with other guests they haven't seen in a while, your family and friends won't be up all night cleaning, and you'll likely save money by holding the wedding at an off-peak time of day and by not feeding guests a full meal. Of course, this means you can get a head start on the honeymoon!

alongside quiches and pastries. Know, though, that because Sunday weddings have become so popular, many vendors are raising their prices. In some locales a brunch (as well as the facility rental costs) may cost just as much as a dinner at a Saturday reception.

Home sweet home. How many times must you hear it, before it starts to sink in, that everything you need may be in your own backyard? If you've exhausted your efforts to find a venue and if your yard or home—or that of your parents or a friend—is able to accommodate your guest list, you may have a reception hall at your ready. The relaxed setting tends to put everyone at ease; the no-rent-required puts your budget at ease. Food can be as simple as a potluck dinner, where relatives and even guests bring a favorite dish. If you want things a bit fancier, hire a caterer. To dress up the surroundings, rent a canopy or tent designed for special events, string some decorative lights around the deck rails, line the entrance with luminarias, and place big pots of flowers or plants in strategic places.

Deck the Hall

If your pocketbook or wallet is threadbare, you'll be happy to hear that you don't need to spend a bunch of money on decorating your reception site. As wedding planner Angie Bloom Hewett puts it: "The wedding ceremony should be beautiful. The rest is just a party."

That said, you don't want guests to walk into a stark, cold-looking room. "As much as it can be beautiful, it should be beautiful," Angie says. Beauty on a budget? Even a theme wedding that requires specific decorations can be done nicely and inexpensively if you use your creativity. (If you opted for a theme wedding in the first place, you're probably creative.) Consider these three penny-pinchers, as well as the ideas in the "More Decorating Dos" **opposite**:

Table talk. At its core, a reception hall is nothing more than a room filled with tables and chairs. As such, wedding planner Alan Dunn recommends making the tables and chairs stand out. You shouldn't have to pay a cent more for colored tablecloths than the standard-issue white, so ask the venue what colors they have. (To be on the safe side, ask if there's an additional charge.) A

More Decorating Dos

If you're planning to decorate your reception site, consider these options, many of which are designed to help you control spending. Also check out the myriad budget-savvy ideas beginning on page 209, which the For Better or For Worse **wedding planners used to dress up reception-hall tables and more.**

- **Think about what's in season (and therefore less expensive). If the reception is in the fall, miniature pumpkins and gourds can adorn tables. In the summer a 99-cent geranium placed in a small clay pot adds natural beauty. In the spring lilacs cut from the trees of family and friends add color and fragrance.**

- **Candles are an inexpensive and elegant touch. Mix tapers, votives, and pillars for a dramatic vignette.**

- **Sprinkle heart-shape confetti on tables. It's a quick way to add color or sparkle.**

- **Pictures are worth a thousand words—and they are a great conversation starter at receptions. Create a picture board of your lives together, starting at childhood. Scan photos into a computer and print them out on heavy paper, along with a brief description of the photo, to create table tents. Photocopy shops and quick-print stores offer a variety of photographic services, such as poster-size prints, that can make fun decorations.**

- **Use clear holiday lights to add sparkle to the room or special tables. Clear lights can also be bundled around a grapevine wreath sitting on the guest-book table or gift table, with a candle placed in the center. Battery-operated strings designed for mantels make it easy to create sparkling centerpieces, without having an electrical source nearby. Borrow lights from friends; wrap masking tape around one end of each string of lights, leaving a tail so you can write the owner's name on the tape.**

- **Shop for decorations in the produce aisle of a supermarket. A bowl of lemons, limes, pears, or apples adds juicy color to guest or serving tables without much expense. Similarly, roadside ditches may be blooming with interesting wildflowers or grasses; just make sure not to pick any state flowers or other plants that are protected by law.**

large hotel may have mahogany chairs that will add richness to a room instead of chrome or white. The bottom line? Ask and you may receive.

Double-duty decorations. We've mentioned this in previous chapters, and we repeat it here: Use the flowers and any other decorations from your ceremony site for the reception. The bride's bouquet can dress the cake table, while the bridesmaids' bouquets can be placed on the head table or serving table. Assign someone to transport flowers and other decorations from the ceremony to the reception, and make sure the person knows exactly where things should be placed.

Mix mastery. There's no reason to feel compelled to deck out every table exactly the same. Matchy-matchy can be boring. Add character by dressing some tables with flowers and others with bowls of fresh fruit. You can decorate tables to reflect your interests (say, fishing-theme tables for him and gardening-theme tables for her) or shared past (mementos from the college you both attended or the bicycle ride where you met). Get friends and relatives into the mix to let them each surprise you with a table. Of course there's an ulterior motive with this almost-anything-goes approach: You can save money. Instead of purchasing 10 dozen matching vases, grab what you have on hand, borrow from friends, or hit local secondhand stores to find one-of-a-kind treasures, as Jackson Lowell did in one episode of **For Better or For Worse**. Skip the florist and pick your own flowers—from the garden or a roadside ditch. If your garden isn't blooming with armfuls of the same flower, pick what you have and place different bouquets on each table. Same-color bouquets are easier to pull off than mixed ones, so make all-white, all-yellow, and all-purple bouquets, for example, and spread color around the room by placing them on alternating tables.

Music to the Ears

ever underestimate the power of some good tunes—and a good musician to get the party going. Whether you want to spend money on a band or DJ is your call; most wedding planners say it's a good idea to offer some type of music. "The music is where the fun comes in," wedding planner Sally Steele says. That, and so much more, she adds. The lead musician or DJ is typically an emcee: He or she is the person who controls the flow of the evening—and gives guests peace of mind—by letting everyone know where to leave gifts, when it's time for the bouquet toss, when the bar is open, and when it's time to go home, among other things.

Review Chapter 3 for guidelines on hiring musicians or a DJ, and the pros and cons of live music versus someone pushing a "play" button. By the time the reception rolls around, you'll also need to clarify these issues:

Play it again. Be specific when it comes to the music you want played. If you've hired a live band, you've obviously selected them because you like what they play. If it's a DJ, the music choices are nearly limitless. Give the DJ a list of songs you want played or access to. Try not to box the person in too much; an experienced DJ will be able to pick up on the vibe of the crowd and improvise here and there. The key is to choose a DJ you trust—someone whom you know won't play a potentially offensive song.

It's a setup. Make sure you know how much setup time the musician or DJ needs for equipment, and that this jives with the hours you have access to the venue.

Time it right. In most cases you want guests to enjoy their meal and dessert while being able to carry on a conversation, so hold off on the music until after the cake is eaten. In some instances, such as a Sunday brunch, soft background music may be appropriate and quite inviting.

Did you hear that? If you're going to the trouble and expense of hiring a musician, make sure guests can hear the person or group. The rhythm of a solo guitarist sitting at the back of a huge room may get lost in the din of guests. On the opposite spectrum are bands or DJs with huge speakers positioned inches away from guests at tables, disrupting conversation.

Food for Thought

Remember back in Chapter 1 when we urged you to set priorities? The food you serve at your reception is a case in point for why that's so important. If you love food (OK, who doesn't? But some couples are more gourmet than others.), you should have earmarked money in your budget for some fantastic spread or mouthwatering cake. If food is way down on your priority list, the potluck reception we've mentioned previously may be in order.

Much of the nitty-gritty about hiring caterers and choosing a menu was covered in Chapter 3, and is worth a look back. If food isn't a priority, skip this section and move on to your priority areas. If you need a little push (or a big shove) to move food higher on your priority list, consider this food for thought from wedding planner Alan Dunn, whose area of expertise is food:

Taste test. True, presentation counts with food. No one will salivate over a grossly lopsided cake with purple icing. But don't be deceived by an overly beautiful cake and pay the big price tag to get it. "I'm so much more for substance than I am style with the cake," Alan says. "Guests will take a peek at the cake, but ultimately what they'll take away from it is the taste. If it's a beautiful cake, but it's a big buttercream mass or it doesn't have a lot of flavor, what's the point? It would make more of an impact to have guests go crazy over how delicious the cake is." The same can be said with the meal and/or appetizers.

Food versus drink. Many eager-to-please couples think a way to a guest's heart is through booze, and they're willing to drop a big chunk of change on it. After all a reception should be a wild party, just a step shy of the bachelor party, right? For Alan, it's the food that's the real crowd pleaser. "The point of the wedding is to celebrate a union. Food is a better way to celebrate than too much alcohol and letting loose. Good food is just a great way to celebrate in general."

Cheap eats. There's no such thing as a free lunch, or a free meal for 500 of your closest friends. But there is such a thing as an affordable meal. For starters keep the menu simple. "Simple doesn't mean bad," Alan says. "Just by simplifying you can save money. You're not going to be able to have lobster, but good chefs should be able to accommodate anybody's palate and budget."

Expert Advice There's no rule that says you have to dole out party favors. "It shouldn't be a perfunctory thing," wedding planner Angie Bloom Hewett says. "Unless you have something really meaningful to give or something sentimental, half of the time guests are going to leave it on the table. I would search my brain for something meaningful, budget for something better, or forgo it all together." An idea she loves: Give a donation to a charity in the name of the guest or guests as a whole. Put the details on a small piece of paper ("In honor of your presence, a donation has been made to ... "), roll it up like a scroll, and leave one at each place setting.

Perception is reality. According to Alan, no matter how lavish the ceremony, attire, flowers, and venue, bad food will leave a bad taste overall. At one seemingly spare-no-expense wedding he attended, the meal had all the flavor of bland airline food. "I'll always think of that wedding as a cheap wedding because of the food," he says. He'd rather chop the guest list and be able to afford a great meal than serve tasteless fare for 600. "The best weddings I have been to all centered around the food," he says.

Personalize It

Too many receptions have a been-there, done-that feel to them. Guests enter a facility with floral centerpieces on every table, a cake table in one corner, and a bar in the other. Unless you spot the bride and groom, guests may not even know if they've landed at the right

For Better
Leave disposable cameras on tables or in a big bowl by the guest book to encourage guests to go wild taking candid photos.

For Worse
Assign five friends to roam the reception with disposable cameras or their own cameras. Buying a boatload of disposable cameras and then developing the film gets costly—plus the results can be iffy because you don't know the picture taker's skills.

reception. With a little ingenuity you can make your reception stand apart from others and put your personal stamp on the event. Cake? Who needs it when a tower of your favorite doughnuts can provide the sugar high? Refer to Chapter 2 for ideas to get you thinking creatively, and also consider these tips for putting a fresh spin on traditional reception elements:

Picture this. The deal often struck with photographers and videographers includes shots of the couple at the head table, cutting the cake, and the first dance. Some guests may be uncomfortable if cameras are rolling while they're at the bar or dancing a jig, so there's no reason to pay for professionals to stick around until midnight. When negotiating what you want (and therefore what you'll have to pay for), think of ways to give your photos and video special flair. Have the photographer snap a photo of the guests seated at each table (before they're shoving food in their mouths), so you have a document of everyone who was there, and then send the photographer home. The videographer can pull guests aside as they arrive and ask them to say a few words—the well wishes are fun to look back on years down the road. (Not everyone is comfortable speaking on camera, so make sure the videographer knows this is a volunteer effort. The wedding party is a good starting point.)

Now that's entertainment. If dancing isn't your thing and you don't mind sharing the spotlight, bring in the clowns—or the mimes or the belly dancers. If you want to stick with traditional music/dance, bring in a ballroom dance instructor for a few hours to teach guests how to waltz or foxtrot. Or how cool is this: Have a celebrity, say Chubby Checker, make a surprise appearance to teach guests the twist. Many celebs or bands who have fallen off the chart are available for private gigs. Yes, you'll still have to pay a pretty penny, but if the addition would make your wildest dreams come true, you may be willing to skimp in other areas. If the celebrity or act happens to be in the area, you can save on travel costs.

Can you do a favor? Where's the heart-shape frame engraved with a couple's names or the little poetry book filled with romantic prose, compliments of brides and grooms who have gone before you? If you a) don't know or b) don't care, consider that a sign that party favors are an area you can nix without anyone feeling they've been cheated out of something.

If you want to give favors, do guests a favor by skipping trite offerings and cheesy knickknacks that they'll feel obligated to display in case you drop by for a visit. Give something that's practical (nearly everyone can use a wineglass, champagne flute, or a candle, assuming you have the money to spend on them—or look at the great champagne flute candles, designed by Alan Dunn, on page 226) or edible. Jordan almonds may be a bit of a yawner, but homemade goodies aren't. If you're known for your chocolate chip cookies, package a few in glassine bags and tie on a bow, along with the recipe. (Bake them ahead of time, package them, and pop them in the freezer for grab-and-go convenience the day of the reception.) A big bowl of mints or bite-size chocolates placed on a table by the exit door can stand in for party favors if you want to give something but simply can't afford much.

Another option for party favors: Hold a drawing to give away the centerpieces or floral arrangements. Though most guests will go home empty-handed, hopefully you've invited people who are mature enough to get over it. And you can always offer up additional slices of cake if you have an abundance of that.

The Order

Just like the pecking order of who waltzes down the aisle first and last at the wedding, there's an order to what happens at the reception. You'll need to tweak things depending upon the formality of the event and your schedule; if you're waiting to take photos after the wedding, for example, you'll need to have the receiving line at the ceremony site or find an alternative way to greet guests. Consider these guidelines for the elements commonly incorporated into the reception:

Receiving line. If you didn't have a receiving line at the ceremony, do it before the reception gets under way. The receiving line should form in the entrance of the reception site so you can greet every guest that comes in the door. Keep things short and sweet: Smile, thank the guest for coming, and move them along down the line. In some cases you can make the transition by turning to introduce the guest to the person standing beside you. See Chapter 5 for more on the receiving line, including who should be in it and the proper order.

Some guests and couples dread a receiving line, with reasons varying from it's too trite and stiff to it causes too much congestion. A modern-minded alternative to a receiving line is for the bride and groom to visit each table after guests have been seated.

Guest seating. In formal gatherings with a sit-down meal, there are often seating charts for guests and place cards on every table. Going that route means extra duties for you: You'll need to think through a seating chart in advance, write it down, have place cards done, and get them on the table. There are also politics to think through: Do you risk a brawl breaking out by placing two super-opinionated relatives next to one another? Would this be the right time to play matchmaker for two single friends? On the other hand, designating where people sit is nice for solo guests who may not know anyone at the reception and for keeping divorced relatives away from one another. If you're more comfortable—and think guests will be too—letting people pick and choose where they sit, you'll save yourself some headaches and expenses. It's not a total free-for-all, though. You'll need to place a reserved sign on a few tables near the head table for immediate family members and, possibly, spouses or guests of the wedding party. To make guests as comfortable as possible, keep tables away from noisy or high-traffic areas, such as kitchen doors, and make sure the chairs are comfortable.

Head table. No one particularly enjoys having people stare at them while they eat, so don't think of the head table in that way. Think of it as merely a tradition that brings order to the reception: When the bride, groom, and attendants are seated at the head table, it's a sign that it's time to eat (though many couples are too sidetracked to really enjoy the meal). The head table is traditionally set off in some way, such as one long table facing the guest tables, and perhaps elevated on a platform. If you'd rather blend in with the crowd, you can designate any table as the head table. With a traditional head table, the bride and groom sit at the center. The best man (or honor attendant) sits next to the bride, and the maid/matron of honor (or honor attendant) sits next to the groom. Other attendants, and often ushers, usually sit at the head table too. If space is an issue, they can be seated at a nearby table.

Toasting. Clink, clink, clink. The sound of someone tapping a glass is sign that it's time for a toast. Toasting is a reception ritual—and one that can easily get carried away (too much clinking, too many slurred speeches from tipsy guests). Tradition dictates that the best man (or groom's honor attendant) gives the first toast. Other toasts are optional. Often the groom gives a toast after the best man (or honor attendant), and then sometimes the bride takes a turn. Parents, usually the fathers, may also want to stand and give their well wishes. See "Toasting Tips" on page 184 for more details. While we're talking toasting, save yourself some money and skip the bride and groom wedding flutes. Ordinary, unadorned flutes work just fine, thank you.

Cake cutting. Guests will know it's time for dessert when the bride and groom make their way to the cake table. The big question: Will they shove the piece of cake into each other's face or gently give one another a bite? Be sure to discuss this as a couple before the big day. It should go without saying that smothering someone's face with cake is a spectacle best left to babies on their first birthday. Save the shenanigans for your honeymoon. Usually the baker or cake server will have at least scored the piece of cake you are to cut off together, so all you have to do is follow the lines. The photographer and videographer can also coach you on what to do.

Dances. If dancing is part of the reception, it's tradition for the first song to be solely for the bride and groom. After that the bride dances with her father, and the groom with his mother, then the wedding party joins in. After that everyone joins in. In some locales a "dollar dance" is held midway through the reception. Guests stand in line to pay a buck to dance with the bride or groom. The ritual can seem tacky, and guests can get carried away, shoving wads of money down the bride's dress or the groom's pants. If you want to keep your reception on a more formal footing, skip this dance.

Garter toss. Tossing the garter is a tradition that has fallen out of favor in today's PC world. Skip it and you can save a few bucks on having to purchase a garter—and likely sneers from women who find it degrading. If you consider it to be harmless fun, schedule the toss toward the end of the reception. The bride sits on a chair in the center of the room or dance floor. The groom slips the garter off the bride's leg and then throws it, over his back, to a group of guys that's assembled. The lucky recipient, tradition holds, is the one who will be the next to marry.

Bouquet toss. Like the garter toss, the bouquet toss has waned somewhat in popularity. Traditionally the bride tosses the bouquet behind her back to a group of single women—many willing to tackle someone to get the thing, as a sign that she will be the next to marry. Plan on having a small, inexpensive bouquet to toss, unless you're willing to part with your real bouquet or you're confident it will land in the hands of someone who will give it back to you. The bouquet toss is done after the garter toss, toward the end of the reception. Often it's a signal the couple is leaving shortly.

Getting Help

There's no reason to wait until the reception day rolls around to realize you can't be everywhere at once or do it all yourself. If the ceremony is taking place on the same day, you may have an appointment with the hair stylist or be headed to the shower about the time you can get into your reception site to decorate. Does the phrase "not enough hours in the day" mean anything to you?

Instead of collapsing from exhaustion or having a meltdown in front of vendors, do what every smart CEO does: delegate. If you don't have a wedding planner (remember, many coordinators can be hired out for just a day) to make sure everything falls into place, take the committee approach by assigning tasks to various individuals. Your perky and reliable aunt can be on hand to get vendors situated, your nieces and nephews can blow up balloons, and your friends can stick around at the end to clean everything up. Ask well in advance if anyone is willing and able to help, including with the yucky stuff like setting up tables and chairs and mopping floors. Choose your helpers wisely: You probably have a good idea of what friends and relatives would take their assignments seriously and which ones are more likely to end up whooping it up on the dance floor or swigging down drinks by the bar. Ultimately how they handle things is a reflection on you.

Toasting Tips

Know when to speak (and when to shut up), stand, or sip with these guidelines for toasting and being toasted.

• To begin making a toast, stand up. Sometimes this will be enough to get guests' attention. If not, gently tap on a glass, pause, and then announce your intention to toast by saying something like, "Ladies and gentlemen, I'm honored to give the first toast." Direct those whom you know will be giving toasts to introduce themselves and tell very briefly how they know you.

• If you have a DJ or musician at the event, consider having that person announce the best man's toast. Depending upon the room size, the people giving a toast may need to borrow the microphone.

• If you're being toasted, stay seated. When the person is finished, smile and nod. Traditionally you do not raise a glass and drink from it at the end of the toast.

• You may need to give the people expected to give toasts some friendly advice beforehand. Politely remind the toasters that you don't want them to share personal details of your once nasty breakup or things that may be offensive to guests or embarrassing to the two of you.

This etiquette also applies to brides and grooms who are toasting parents. Don't talk about how you had to pinch pennies because they couldn't afford to chip in for the wedding. Always accentuate the positive.

• A toast isn't a speech. Limit it to four minutes tops.

• If you want to keep the toasting from spiraling out of control, with guest after guest making pronouncements, have the best man or father of the bride make that clear in his toast. He can politely say something like, "Bob and Mary are anxious to talk to all of you who've come here to support them, so let's dispense with the toasting so the mingling and dancing can begin."

• To kiss or not to kiss? In some places tapping on glasses signifies that guests want the bride and groom to smooch. The clinking can get annoying, not to mention that guests can get carried away and end up breaking glasses that you'll ultimately pay for. Try something different: Request that those who want you two to kiss must sing a song about love. It's a fun departure from the expected!

Certain responsibilities traditionally fall on certain people. The best man (or groom's honor attendant), for example, is usually the one who makes sure vendors get their payments. Those guidelines are covered in Chapter 1; take a look back to refresh your memory.

Here's the deal: There's no reason to keep anyone in the dark about what's expected of them. Your attendants may be wondering if they'll be sitting at the head table or if they can hook up with their old college buddies who will also be attending. After you have everyone on board—attendants, balloon blowers, and so forth—make a list of responsibilities and an itinerary for the reception (see "Reception Timeline," page 186), similar to what you already did for the ceremony (see "Ceremony Itinerary," page 160). Though you don't have to account for every minute, establishing a general timeline will help everything run more efficiently and take the guesswork out of who's doing what. Perhaps more importantly a timeline puts an end to things. If you let the champagne flow longer than you originally agreed on or ask the DJ to stick around a few extra hours, you'll end up paying overtime charges—often including for the facility and any help it has provided.

Final Thoughts

Years ago parting was such sweet sorrow. The bride changed into a getaway dress, grabbed the groom's hand, and the newlyweds dashed out through a throng of cheering guests, leaving weepy-eyed parents in the dust. It made sense, or so it seemed, to counter a grand entrance at a wedding with a dramatic exit at the reception.

The drama usually unfolds differently today. Many couples stay until the bitter end, then grab a mop and broom to help clean up the joint—not exactly a Cinderella ending, but a reality for many. Other couples change into casual clothes and quietly slip out a back door (if you do this, make sure you say a quick goodbye and thank-you to immediate family members and key helpers). Still couples who aren't too pooped to keep partying may decide to join guests for a night on the town. (continued on page 190)

Reception Timeline

To ensure that everything for your reception gets done, make an itinerary showing a time frame for when various elements need to be started. Complete this list to give order to your party and to catch any things you've forgotten (such as asking your aunt to serve the cake!). Use the information to make an informal agenda to distribute to pertinent parties several weeks before your wedding. (Also make sure to bring extra copies on the day of the wedding.) If appropriate, note the person responsible for making sure the task gets done and include cell phone numbers.

Pre-Reception Tasks

- Setup (tables, chairs, etc.) begins at: _____

- Decorating begins at: _____

- Florist arrives at: _____

- Food/caterer arrives at: _____

- Cake arrives at: _____

- Bar is set up at: _____

- Musician sets up equipment at:
  _____

- Person(s) in charge of overseeing the pre-reception tasks: _____

Reception

- Receiving line forms at: _____

- People in receiving line are:
  _____
  _____
  _____
  _____

- Appetizers, punch/drinks ready to be served at: _____

- Person(s) serving are: _____

- Guest book is in place by:
  _____

- Guest-book attendant and/or person transporting guest book from ceremony is: _____

- Flowers from wedding are in place by: _____

- Person responsible for moving flowers from ceremony to reception is: _____

- Photographer/videographer arrives at: _____

- Formal photos are taken at:
  _____

- Head table and guests are seated by: _____
  _____
  _____

People sitting at head table are:

_____

_____

_____

_____

_____

_____

_____

_____

People sitting at reserved tables by head table are: _____

Servers arrive at: _____

Meal starts at: _____

Meal is completed by: _____

Bride and groom cut cake/take photos at: _____

Cake is served at: _____

Person cutting the cake is:

_____

DJ/musicians arrive at: _____

Music begins at: _____

Couple's first dance begins at:

_____

Couple leaves reception at:

_____

Dance/reception ends at:

_____

Other: _____

_____

_____

_____

_____

Post-Reception Tasks

Tear down (remove decorations, take down tables, etc.):

_____

Flowers go to: _____

Person in charge of this: _____

Leftover food goes to: _____

Person in charge of this: _____

Leftover cake goes to (if you are planning to freeze the top of the cake to eat on your first anniversary, make plans for this): _____

Person in charge of this is:

_____

Pay musician, other vendors at:

_____

Person in charge of this is:

_____

Name, address, and phone number of reception site:

_____

_____

_____

_____

_____

_____

Sample Reception Itinerary

**Reception Itinerary and Tasks
for the wedding of John Smith
and Jane Doe**

**Location: XYZ Community Hall,
555 5th St., Anytown, Arizona
Date: Saturday, July 23, 2005**

**Pre-Reception Tasks
10 a.m.–4 p.m.
Set up tables and chairs;
decorate; pick up floral
arrangements; help caterers and
baker get situated.**

**Jill Doe is in charge of the pre-
reception tasks and meeting with
vendors on the day of the
wedding. Her cell phone number
is 555/555-5555. Others helping
her are Bob Doe, John Doe,
Angie and Kevin Smith, and
Sue Miller.**

**The contact for the facility site is
MaryAnne Hanson. Her phone
number is 555/555-5556.**

**11 a.m.
Florist arrives.**

**3 p.m.
Caterers arrive.**

**4 p.m.
DJ arrives to set up equipment.**

Baker arrives with cake.

**Reception
6 p.m.–6:30 p.m.
Receiving line forms at entrance
(for bride, groom, and parents).**

Bar opens.

**Attendants can leave personal
belongings in the room at the
back of the facility.**

**6:30 p.m.
Guests are seated at tables.
Wedding party and immediate
family are seated at head table
and reserved tables. (Due to
space limitations, only the bride,
groom, and two honor attendants
will be at the head table. Other
attendants, ushers, and their
spouses/guests will find seating at
the reserved tables near the
head table.)**

Servers offer champagne.

**Best man (or honor attendant)
makes toast after everyone
is seated.**

Groom makes toast.

Officiant offers blessing.

Servers begin serving the meal.

**7:30 p.m.
Bride's father makes toast.**

**Bride and groom cut cake/take
photos.**

**Servers begin clearing tables and
serving cake.**

**7:45 p.m.
Dance begins.**

Best man gives envelopes with payments for caterer/servers.

9:45 p.m.
Groom throws garter/bride tosses bouquet.

10 p.m.
Dance/reception ends.

Couple leaves for hotel.

Post-Reception Tasks
10 p.m.
Best man gives envelope with payment for DJ.

Best man and maid of honor gather gifts and guest book; deliver to bride's parents' home.

Couple's parents to tend to any leftover food and cake.

Cleanup crew takes down decorations, tables, and chairs, and does light cleaning of facility. Jill Doe is in charge of the post-reception tasks and meeting with vendors on the day of the wedding. Others helping her are Bob Doe, John Doe, Angie and Kevin Smith, and Sue Miller. Anyone else who is able to help out would be appreciated.

Thank you for making our day special and helping it run so smoothly! We couldn't have done it without you!

How long you stay at the reception and how you choose to exit is up to you. Of course it would look rude if you walked out as soon as you finished the meal, so don't book a flight for your honeymoon an hour into the reception. (If your honeymoon is that important to you, it's better to put your money into it instead of a reception you'd rather not be at. Maybe an hour-long cake-and-punch shindig is really all you wanted? Reread Chapter 1 to make sure you have your priorities straight.)

It's equally rude to leave without tying up loose ends—or at least giving instructions to trusted friends and relatives on what needs to be done. Some considerations before you flee the scene:

Pay pal. Make sure all vendors are paid, or that arrangements have been made for payment after the reception. As stated in previous chapters, the best man (or groom's honor attendant) is usually in charge of this. The bride's father or other trusted friend or relative can also handle the payments, with instruction (and money) from you, of course. As you can imagine, it's not fun to stop and write a check for the florist during your first dance.

Expert Advice **Enough already!**
Don't drag your reception out until the wee hours, long after weary guests have started routinely checking their watches. "Let your event end on a high note," wedding planner Angie Bloom Hewett says. "Nobody wants to be at your wedding until 2 in the morning. Let them leave thinking this is the best event they ever attended."

Leftovers again? Determine in advance what should be done with leftovers. Even if you've hired someone to cater it, you'll likely pay for it, so there's no reason to let it go to waste. Out-of-town guests may appreciate a container to put in their hotel fridge for a midnight snack, or your parents may need every morsel to feed the guests who've invaded their homes. Donating to a homeless center is another option; make sure you have the arrangements for delivery worked out in advance. Homes for troubled youths or for senior citizens may enjoy being treated to the cake you couldn't get rid of.

Room to bloom. If you brought the flowers used at the wedding to the reception site, good for you. You've pinched pennies! Now the question is what to do with the flowers. You can give them to a special guest or helper. Or you can make a game out of it by having a drawing at the end of the reception; the guests whose names are drawn from a bowl go home with the arrangements. Donating the flowers to a church, hospital, or care facility is always a nice gesture.

Clean sweep. If cleaning up is part of the deal with the venue, it's best to have a crew intact rather than leaving it to chance that your in-laws will be happy to do the dirty work. Get a few responsible friends and relatives to commit to staying afterwards to take down decorations, return rental items, spruce things up, turn out the lights, and lock the doors. Appoint one person as the foreman/forewoman, and make sure that person has a list of what needs to be done, as well as where the food, flowers, and so forth are to go.

The Perfect

Think you're finished? Not quite!

Ending

Find out how to wrap up the final details.

chapter
7

And they lived happily ever after ...

Sigh. That storybook ending has such a nice ring to it. After all the planning, pomp, and circumstance you'll be more than ready to ride off into the sunset to begin your happily ever after. For some couples that means hightailing it out to begin the honeymoon. For others it means hitting the sack at home for a few hours and dragging themselves out of bed for a postwedding brunch the in-laws are hosting.

How you choose to put closure on your wedding is up to you. Well, at least some of it is. You can decide if and when you want to take a honeymoon, and if you want to invite everyone over to watch you open gifts. Other things, such as paying bills and writing thank-you notes, are less flexible. You need a deadline so you don't put them off and ruin your credit rating, your good name, or both.

A job well done doesn't happen if details are left undone. This last leg is painless, but it's just as important as the first details that may seem so long, long ago.

The Honeymoon

Just like weddings, anything goes with honeymoons. You can go where you want—fly to another country or drive to a B&B 20 miles away—and when you want. There's no rule that says the honeymoon must begin as soon as the wedding bands are on the fingers. If you've exhausted your finances, and quite possibly yourselves, putting off the honeymoon is a smart idea. Consider these ideas and guidelines for your honeymoon—whatever form that comes in:

The quickie honeymoon. There's no reason that you have to subscribe to the typical image of "honeymoon." If time and money aren't on your side, make it short and sweet. Steal away for a one-night stay in a local hotel. A weekend getaway to a B&B, a cabin in the woods, or a nearby city is another way to have an enjoyable and affordable honeymoon. Even if you have to retreat to your own home, you can make it special by having a bottle of chilled champagne waiting for you. The important thing is to have a little bit of time alone to decompress. If you want you can start saving your money for a bigger honeymoon on your first anniversary.

The real deal. If you're up to the task of a full-fledged honeymoon right after the marriage and you've budgeted for it, more power to you. Make the most of the trip by putting the wedding details out of your mind and focusing on your lives together. Don't bring along the thank-you cards, thinking you'll scribble them out on the plane or as you're watching the sunset. Forget about trying to nab the rolls of film from your relatives' cameras before you leave, and then finding a one-hour developer on the remote island you're staying at. You'll have plenty of time for that stuff when you get home. What you do need to worry about, at least during the wedding planning, is to find a place you'll both enjoy (ask friends for ideas, and let a travel agent book the trip). Gather any necessary documents, such as passports or birth certificates, sooner rather than later. Pack your bags the week before the wedding, so you're not scrambling at the last minute, and make sure driver's licenses, passports, credit cards, and so forth are in a carry-on bag.

Quick Tip Don't book the honeymoon suite in the same hotel where you've booked rooms for the guests. No matter how much you love them, you'll want some breathing room at the end of the night. Plus you don't want to run the risk of chatty (or inebriated) guests knocking on your door at all hours.

A family affair. With second marriages and blended families, a honeymoon can take on an entirely new look and feel. It may be an ideal time for the kids to really get to know one another, so bring them along and call it a family vacation. It's still a good idea, though, for Mom and Dad to have some time alone. See if a relative can babysit for a day or two after the wedding and spend the time alone together in a local hotel or nearby site. Then gather up the brood for the longer honeymoon/family vacation.

A final note about the honeymoon: Be sure to leave your contact information, including any flight information, with parents or other dependable sources. The era of making the honeymoon destination top secret has long passed. People need to know where you are in case of an emergency.

Thank-You Notes

e've said it before, and we'll say it again: You can never say thanks too many times. Barring a sudden act of Congress, there's no law that says you have to send thank-you notes for all the gifts and help you received. But fortunately most couples are astute enough to realize it's good manners to do so.

The sooner you get the thank-you notes sent, the better. Etiquette says you have one month after the ceremony to get it done. If you're waiting to open gifts at a party three weeks after the wedding, you can still get the thank-yous going. As soon as possible after the wedding, send a thanks to attendants, parents, grandparents, and others who went above and beyond. You can even start addressing the envelopes before the wedding for people who may have already sent a gift—even if you haven't yet opened it.

Refer to the "Invitations and Stationery" section, page 86, in Chapter 3 for more details on thank-you notes. As mentioned previously the important thing is to get the thank-you cards done, not to fret over whether they perfectly match your invitations or wedding programs. Cards purchased from a discount store are perfectly acceptable, and homemade cards—which can be made inexpensively—show guests how much you really care.

Now what do you say and how? Use these tips:

Get organized. To keep from forgetting anyone or from sending two thank-yous to the same person, you need a system. Find a system that works for you—for instance, use the "Invitations" checklist on page 206 or print out a spreadsheet if you've been keeping track of everything on your computer—and set it up before you dive into the stack of thank-yous that needs to be done.

Divvy them up. The bride can write the thank-yous for the people she knows best, and the groom for his friends.

Work in shifts. Don't block off an entire day; you'll only end up with cramps in your hand. Twenty minutes every day is a more realistic approach.

Handwrite the notes. Even if your penmanship isn't perfect, a handwritten note is much more personal than a computer-generated one. Purchase a black pen that writes smoothly and that's comfortable in your hand.

Be specific. If you've ever received a thank-you note that reads "Thank you for the gift," it may have left you wondering if the recipient knew what the gift was or if he or she wrote out all the cards in advance. Don't be vague. Mention the gift specifically ("Thank you for the blender."). If the gift is money, you don't need to mention the exact amount. Always make an effort to mention how you'll use the gift. For example, "We both love margaritas, so the blender is perfect!" Even if you hate the gift or you've already received 10 of them, be gracious. A little white lie doesn't hurt.

Don't Forget ...

 our to-do list is getting shorter and shorter and shorter. Before long you can crumple it up and toss it in the trash. Consider these the final chapters in your wedding book:

Wedding announcement. The engagement announcement guidelines in Chapter 1 apply to wedding announcements, so refer back to those. Some newspapers have time frames for how long after the wedding they'll publish announcements; others take them at any time because you have to pay for the announcement. Find out the details in advance. You'll also need to know if the newspaper accepts black and white, color, or either type of photography, and whether they will accept a digital image. Newspapers have varying degrees of technology, so what works for one may not work for another.

Bills. You've been paying them all along, and the bills may seem to be on a never-ending cycle even after the reception. Pay up! The sooner you can get them out of the way, the sooner you can get on with being husband and wife. If you stayed within your budget, there should be no surprises.

Name change. Oops! There's been more than one bride who has forgotten to change her name after taking her groom's last name—or vice versa. The little things—like the name plaque hanging outside your cubicle or the labels you use to send bills—are harmless enough. But the big things—Social Security records, driver's license, retirement accounts, insurance policies, and wills, for example— need your attention pronto. Refer to Chapter 3, "Legal Details," page 121, for more on that subject.

Marriage certificate. As mentioned previously the officiant or licensed authority who married you is typically in charge of getting the signed marriage certificate filed with the appropriate authority. To be on the safe side, clarify that he or she will handle this important matter. Nine times out of ten, the certificate gets filed promptly after the ceremony, in accordance with the laws of the state in which you were married. Make sure the mailing address you'll be residing at after the ceremony is on the appropriate paperwork and any return envelope. You should receive a certified copy of the certificate a few weeks after the ceremony. If you don't, call the county clerk's office, vital statistics registrar, or the appropriate authority in your state to check the status. A quick call to the officiant may clear up matters—hopefully the document isn't forgotten under a stack of papers. There's often a 90-day filing period, so the delay doesn't mean you have to have a do-over, but it does point out the importance of knowing the legal deadlines in your state. As mentioned in Chapter 2, if you get married abroad, get a certified copy of the certificate before you leave. After everything you've been through, you don't want it to be all for naught, do you?

Dress. If you purchased a bridal gown and you plan to keep it, you'll have to pay to preserve it. If you paid $100 for the dress, is it worth it to pay more than that to have it professionally cleaned, pressed, and boxed—and then finding a place to stash it? (See why selling the dress isn't such a bad idea after all?) Most dry cleaners offer a service where they'll lay the gown and accessories in acid-free papers, positioning the bodice in a clear window of the box so you can gasp at the beauty whenever you need a little princess pick-me-up. Plan to pay at least $150 for such a service; call around to dry cleaners in your area to find the best deal. You can also box it yourself, using acid-free papers to help prevent damage or discoloration, and then sealing the box to keep critters out. If you're not too concerned about preserving the dress as a monument for future generations, just put it in a garment bag and hang it in the closet or stash it in a trunk like great-great-grandma did.

Final Thoughts

Imagine regaining your life—no more talks about tablecloths and place settings, no more waking up in a panic at 2 a.m. in fear that you left someone's name off the wedding program. At long last, a return to normalcy (well, as normal as it can be when you're essentially starting a brand-new phase of your life).

Don't fear if it takes some time to come down from your wedding high. The weeks and months following the wedding will still be filled with banter about your nuptials. People will be asking to see pictures, wondering about the gifts you've received, and inquiring about your wedded bliss.

Go ahead and indulge in the postwedding hoopla. (You wouldn't want to go cold turkey, anyway, would you?) Tote a mini wedding album around and share it with everyone. Dish about the great gifts you received. Heck, even reward yourself for staying on budget by plucking $50 from a few cards you received and treating yourselves to a massage or a quiet dinner. Give yourself a pat on the back; you deserve it!

We

Work

Keep track of your budget, with these easy-

book

plan your menu, and more to-use worksheets.

chapter 8

Budget Breakdown

Pencil in the estimated costs of these common expenses, and then revisit this worksheet to keep a tally of your wedding till. Cross out any categories that don't pertain to your wedding—and use the "other" category to list items specific to your celebration.

Item	Estimated Cost	Actual Cost

Pre-Wedding

Item	Estimated Cost	Actual Cost
Stationery (invitations, guest book)	$ _____	$ _____
Postage	$ _____	$ _____
Engagement announcement in newspaper	$ _____	$ _____
Wedding rings	$ _____	$ _____
Marriage license	$ _____	$ _____
Other _____	$ _____	$ _____

Wedding Day

Item	Estimated Cost	Actual Cost
Bridal gown	$ _____	$ _____
Veil	$ _____	$ _____
Shoes and accessories	$ _____	$ _____
Bridal bouquet for carrying	$ _____	$ _____
Bridal bouquet for tossing	$ _____	$ _____
Groom's attire	$ _____	$ _____
Bridesmaids' attire	$ _____	$ _____
Bridesmaids' bouquets	$ _____	$ _____
Groomsmen's attire	$ _____	$ _____
Wedding party boutonnieres and corsages	$ _____	$ _____

Item	Estimated Cost	Actual Cost
Attendant/helper gifts	$ _____	$ _____
Photography	$ _____	$ _____
Videography	$ _____	$ _____
Ceremony site	$ _____	$ _____
Ceremony site decorations	$ _____	$ _____
Officiant	$ _____	$ _____
Wedding music/musicians	$ _____	$ _____
Transportation	$ _____	$ _____
Reception site	$ _____	$ _____
Reception site decorations	$ _____	$ _____
Food/caterer	$ _____	$ _____
Cake	$ _____	$ _____
Drinks	$ _____	$ _____
Reception music	$ _____	$ _____
Guest favors	$ _____	$ _____
Gratuities	$ _____	$ _____
Other _____	$ _____	$ _____

Post-Wedding

Item	Estimated Cost	Actual Cost
Honeymoon	$ _____	$ _____
Wedding announcement in newspaper	$ _____	$ _____
Thank-you cards	$ _____	$ _____
Postage	$ _____	$ _____
Photos/album	$ _____	$ _____
Wedding gown cleaning/storage	$ _____	$ _____
Other _____	$ _____	$ _____
Total Costs	$ _____	$ _____

Contact Information

Do you need an easy way to keep track of vendors who are supplying goods and services on your wedding day? Photocopy this "business card" to stay organized and keep everything you need at your fingertips.

Wedding role (florist, bridesmaid, DJ, etc.) _____

Name _____

Position _____

Company _____

Phone _____

Cell phone _____

Fax _____

Address _____

E-mail _____

Website _____

Notes _____

_____

_____

_____

Menu Planning

Use this list to jot down ideas for your reception menu.

Appetizers _____

_____

Beverages _____

_____

Bar selections _____

_____

Main entrée(s) _____

_____

Side dishes _____

_____

Desserts _____

_____

Wedding cake _____

     Size _____

     Shape _____

     Flavor _____

     Icing _____

     Topper _____

     Number served _____

Invitations

Photocopy this list to keep track of who is coming, gifts received, and thank-you cards sent.

Name _____

Address _____

City _____

State _____

ZIP _____

Invitation sent _____

RSVP received _____

Number attending _____

Meal preference, if applicable _____

Gift received _____

Thank-you note sent _____

Clothing Measurements

Having your measurements on hand—and those of your wedding party—will make shopping for attire at a bridal shop, consignment shop, or online faster and easier. Make sure you have a professional do the measuring to ensure a comfortable fit for all garments. Photocopy the following charts for everyone who requires special attire for the wedding day.

Bride/Female Attendants/Mother of Bride/Mother of Groom/Flower Girl

Dress size _____

Shoe size _____

Bust _____

Waist _____

Hips _____

Skirt length _____

Waist to _____ **inches above floor** _____

Sleeve length _____

(continued on page 208)

Groom/Male Attendants/Father of Bride/Father of Groom/Ring Bearer/Ushers

Jacket size _____

Shoe size _____

Chest _____

Neck _____

Hips _____

Waist _____

Inseam _____

Sleeve length _____

Shoulder to wrist _____

Themes & Ideas

Dozens of great theme and project ideas from the For Better or For Worse **wedding professionals.**

Alecia Davis

Alan Dunn

Angie Bloom Hewett

Jackson Lowell

Matt O'Dorisio

Erika Shay

Sally Steele

Fairy Tale

Angie Bloom Hewett

Angie planned this fit-for-a-prince-and-princess affair for one lucky couple. From start—a runner that read "And they lived happily ever after ..."—to finish—a luscious cake with a miniature version of Cinderella's carriage as a topper—this celebration had all the elements of a modern-day fairy tale.

Use these ideas to make your fairy-tale fantasies come true: a slipper-topped centerpiece, a cake covered with icing ropes and roses, gold-tipped roses in the bride's bouquet, and menu cards embellished with miniature slippers.

Instructions on page 242.

Groovy '60s

Matt O'Dorisio

Add some flower power to your wedding day with colors and motifs reminiscent of the hip, happening 1960s. Frame the altar with swaths of fabric in eye-popping hues, dress up the aisle with a brightly patterned runner, and choose flowers in unconventional colors for spirited bouquets.

Love color? Then this groovy scheme may be your rescue from been-there-done-that themes: Create Warhol-esque posters to display, and make programs with paper, decorative hole punches, and glue sticks—fast and cheap! Don't want to scream theme? Just select candy-colored flowers for fun bouquets.

Instructions on page 248.

1950s Cuba

Jackson Lowell

Create a tropical feel without leaving home with these great ideas: Display rolled programs to resemble cigars, use homemade "palm trees" to dress up tables, and let your guests try their luck at casino-style games.

Instructions on page 232.

Alan Dunn

Inspired by the colors and imagery of a faraway land, Alan created an Arabian fantasy with attire fit for a prince and princess, easy-to-make pillows for guests to lounge on, and bejeweled genie-bottle centerpieces complete with dry ice.

I Dream of Jeannie

An Affair to Remember

Alan Dunn

Classic color schemes need not be boring. Treat guests to candle favors, and create simply stunning bouquets and more to dress up the theme.

Instructions on page 226.

Instructions on page 241.

If you have a sweet tooth, let it guide the look of your big day. For this celebration, a photographer's studio was transformed into a sweet retreat with vinyl dots affixed to the floor, custom candies, and edible confetti for the guests to throw instead of traditional rice.

Candy Land

Bouquets

A bride's bouquet can take many forms—as can those of her attendants. Here are some money-saving ideas you can make today.

Instructions on page 246.

Instructions on page 244.

A lei (for both the bride and groom) is the perfect adornment for a seaside wedding, while hand-tied bouquets are suitable for any type of wedding.

Instructions on page 243.

Altars and Ceremony Decorations

Instructions on page 240.

Indoors or out, the focus of the ceremony should be on the bride and groom. Flower-covered arches are popular options, but a "window frame" is unexpected and equally stunning. A chuppah is traditionally used for Jewish ceremonies.

Instructions on page 238.

Instructions on page 228.

Great Ideas

Decorations

Instructions on page 230.

The sky's the limit when it comes to decorating your event with style. A Zenlike fountain can add a calming feel to an Asian-inspired event, while a "wishing tree" is a beautiful addition to any ceremony. If you have a hobby, such as playing pool, let your decorations reflect it.

Instructions on page 236.

Instructions on page 235.

Cakes

Cakes are the delicious finishing touch to the reception meal—a great way to say thanks to your guests for joining you on your special day.

Frosting flourishes aren't your only option: You can decorate your cake with flowers, tall filled cookies, or candy-hued fondant.

Great Ideas

Invitations and Programs

There's no need to spend hundreds—or thousands—on the invitations, ceremony programs, menu cards, and thank-you notes for your wedding. Consider these inexpensive ideas from the For Better or For Worse wedding planners.

Courtney and G... ...r Tying the Knot!

Love is patient, love is kind. It does not envy, it does not boast, it is not proud. It is not rude, it is not self-seeking, it is not easily angered, it keeps no record of wrongs. Love does not delight in evil but rejoices with the truth. It always protects, always trusts, always hopes, always perseveres.

Paul & Lisa

Sunday, the 21st Day of March 2004

Pretty paper tied with a bow, groovy designs created with a child's spin art machine, and a felt-backed tile are all great do-it-yourself options.

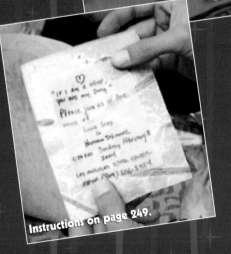

Instructions on page 250.

Paper stenciled with a lacy pattern, a seashell with a freehand message, and handmade "paper" are additional budget-savvy ideas.

With Joyful Hearts We Celebrate the Wedding of Sasha & Eddie August 30th 4:00 P.M. Malibu, California

Instructions on page 249.

Centerpieces

Dress the tables at your reception to the nines with these great ideas.

Cigar boxes filled with flowers have a tropical feel, while tall, narrow arrangements are stunning and don't prevent guests from conversing across the table. A handmade lava lamp is a fun alternative to an ordinary arrangement.

Instructions on page 234.

Projects

Money-saving projects you can create with ease!

chapter
9

Champagne Flute Candles

$5 for 6 candles

Designed by Alan Dunn

Candles add a romantic glow to any reception setting—and these easy-to-make candles are no exception. The candles, shown on page 216, are a golden champagne color, but use whatever color best complements your wedding-day color scheme.

You Will Need

- 21-ply flat braid wick
- Six ½" metal washers
- 2 lb. of 140 wax
- ½ gallon of water
- Double boiler
- ½ yellow or other color dye chip
- Vybar*

- Vanilla or other scent
- 6 champagne flutes
- Drop cloth, scissors, sticky notes, needle, hammer, stir stick, teaspoon, oven mitts, pitcher, clean rag

*This preservative locks in the scent and color of the wax.

1 Place the drop cloth on your work surface.

2 Cut six wicks, each 9 inches long. Thread each wick through a metal washer; tie a slipknot at the end of each wick to keep the wick secured to the washer. Poke a hole in the center of each sticky note with the needle.

3 Using the hammer, break the 2-pound wax block into small pieces.

4 Boil the water in the pot of the double boiler. Put the pieces of wax in the pan on the double boiler. Melt the wax, stirring until all pieces of wax are dissolved and form a liquid.

5 Add the dye chip, 1 teaspoon of Vybar, and 1 teaspoon of vanilla scent to the liquid wax. Stir until the dye chip and Vybar have completely dissolved.

6 Wearing oven mitts, carefully pour the liquid wax into the pitcher. Carefully pour wax into the champagne flutes, filling them about 1 inch from the rim. **Note: Wipe up any spills and splashes on the outside of the glasses immediately with a clean rag; otherwise the wax will dry and will be difficult to remove.**

7 Drop one wick into each flute so that the washer rests at the bottom of the glass. Thread each wick through the center of a sticky note to hold the wick in the center of the flute. Let the candles harden overnight.

8 Cut any excess wick from the top of the candle.

Options
Here are some great ways to further personalize these candles:

• **Create a computer-generated or handwritten note—thanking your guests for sharing in your celebration. Attach the note with ribbon to the stem of the glass.**

• **Etch your guests' initials onto the glasses with inexpensive, easy-to-use etching cream, available at crafts stores.**

• **Add some sparkle to the glasses by adhering faux crystals to the glasses with superstrong adhesive.**

Decorative Chuppah

$81

Designed by Sally Steele

The chuppah signifies the new home the newlyweds will soon share. This version, shown on page 219, is made of organza fabric and adorned with fringe. The chuppah can be used inside or out. Mazel Tov!

You Will Need

- 3 yards 52"-wide organza fabric, ivory

- 3 yards 3½"-long fringe, ivory

- 4 feet 1½"-wide satin ribbon, ivory

- 4 wooden poles, each 8 feet long and 1½" diameter

- 4 umbrella stands*

- 4 eyelet hooks

- 11 yards 1½"-wide satin ribbon, red

- Optional: 10 red carnations, monofilament thread, crafts needle

- Pin, needle, thread, hot-glue gun, glue sticks, scissors

*If you don't have umbrella stands, you can either stick the poles into the ground or make stands using containers filled with quick-setting cement. See Step 4.

1 Finish the edges of the organza by turning the edges under ½ inch; pin in place and hand-stitch.

2 Apply hot glue to one 3-yard-long edge of the organza; this will be the front edge. Adhere the fringe to the organza.

3 Cut four pieces of ivory satin ribbon, each 1 foot long. Fold each piece of ribbon in half and hand-stitch the center (folded portion) of each piece to a corner of the fabric, leaving the two ends free.

4 Place each wooden pole into an umbrella stand. Screw each eyelet hook into the end of each wooden pole.

5 Thread each ivory satin ribbon through an eyelet hook so that the fabric hangs like a canopy on top of the wooden poles.

6 Cut four pieces of red satin ribbon, each 8 feet long. Loop one ribbon through each eyelet hook; tie to secure. Start at the top of each ribbon and crisscross the ribbon around the poles to the bottom; tie the ends to the poles to secure.

7 Optional: Remove the stems of the carnations with the scissors. Using monofilament thread and the crafts needle, string five carnations together to hang from the top of one front pole; repeat for the other pole.

The Chuppah Tradition

Long ago a newly married couple consummated their marriage in the groom's tent, or chuppah. Today the couple stands under the chuppah with the rabbi during the wedding ceremony to represent their new home. The four poles represent pillars of trust and faith, on which the marriage must stand.

Traditionally parents plant trees when their children are born—cypress for girls and cedar for boys. When the children are married, branches from the trees are used for the chuppah.

Zen Fountain

$50

Designed by Matt O'Dorisio

Nothing sets a more relaxing tone at a ceremony or reception than water—and this Zen fountain fits the bill perfectly. Place a pair of fountains where guests enter the ceremony or reception site, or place them near the gift or cake table. While fountains such as this design, featured on page 220, work well for an Asian-theme celebration, your choice of decorative bowl can easily match the tone of any theme.

You Will Need

- Small (approx. 2"×3") garden fountain pump

- Ceramic or glass fountain bowl, deep enough to bury your pump*

- Plastic hose in diameter that fits the pump

- Decorative rocks

- Several bamboo rods in a diameter that will fit the hose

- Twine

- Scissors, handsaw, water

*If your chosen bowl has a drain hole in the base, plug it with silicone; let dry.

1 Place the fountain pump in the bottom of the bowl. Cut enough plastic hose to reach from the pump to the top of the bowl. Attach one end of the hose to the pump; cut the hose so that it is about 6 inches taller than the top of the bowl.

2 Pile the decorative rocks on top of the pump, taking care to keep the pump upright and the connection to the hose intact.

3 Using the handsaw, cut one bamboo rod to a length that spans from the pump to the top of the bowl. Connect the end of the hose to the end of the rod. Bury the connection between the plastic hose and the bamboo

rod under the decorative rocks already in the bowl, securing the rod upright (so the water will go straight up through the rod and bubble up and over the end).

4 Cut the remaining bamboo rods of varying heights; cluster them around the rod/hose. Secure with twine.

5 Fill the bowl with water; plug in the pump. **Note: If the fountain doesn't flow, ensure all connections are secure.**

Fountain Project Option

The fountain designed by Matt O'Dorisio uses decorative rocks to conceal the pump and hose; however, you can also create a "living" fountain with potted plants and fish to later display in your garden or on your deck or porch.

• Plug any drainage holes with a rubber-gasketed, stainless-steel bolt or a piece of liner spread with caulk. Seal any minor cracks in the chosen container with caulk or brush on water garden sealant.

• To grow fish and plants, add an aquarium bubbler or a spitter fountain to oxygenate the water. Conceal the cord and plug it into a ground-fault-interrupted outlet.

• Fill the container with water. Place bricks that will raise the level of the pots of aquatic plants. Before planting or stocking with fish, let the water sit for five to seven days.

• Add potted plants on supports so that the tops of the pots will be below the water surface. Then add floating plants.

• Allow fish to adjust gradually to the water temperature by leaving them in their original water in a plastic bag. After 10 minutes, release the fish.

Palm Tree Decoration

$75

Designed by Jackson Lowell

This lush, exotic decoration, shown on page 214, will add visual flavor to any tropical-theme event, inside or out. It can be placed on a table—such as a buffet or gift table—or stand near the altar for interesting height and drama.

You Will Need

- 3 bamboo rods, each 5 feet long

- Twine

- Floral foam*

- Heavy foam planter

- Large bundle of banana leaves

- Large bundle of palm leaves

- 3 large monkey tails

- Various tropical flowers, such as birds-of-paradise

- 1 dozen roses

- Scissors, bucket of water

*Floral foam is commonly known as Oasis (a brand name); look for this product at crafts stores.

1 Form a tripod with the bamboo rods; make a "cradle" in the top of the tripod that will hold the foam planter.

2 Wrap twine around the top of the tripod where the poles meet; cut and tie to secure.

3 Soak the floral foam in water for 20 minutes. Place the floral foam inside the foam planter; the foam should rise out of the planter so it is easier to insert the leaves and flowers. Place the foam planter inside the top "cradle" of the tripod.

4 Insert the banana and palm leaves into the floral foam, spacing them so that the leaves resemble a palm tree. Insert the monkey tails into the floral foam. Insert the tropical flowers into the floral foam, filling any gaps between the leaves and monkey tails.

5 Insert a cluster of roses in the center front portion of the floral foam, trimming the stems if needed.

"Drama, huh? This is more of the tropics that we are going to bring from Havana."
—Jackson Lowell to his team when presenting this project idea.

For additional ideas that suit a 1950s Cuban theme, including rolled wedding programs that resemble cigars, see page 214.

Lava Lamp Centerpiece

$37

Designed by Matt O'Dorisio

Want to add a groovy touch to your reception? This fun and funky centerpiece, featured on page 224, resembles a lava lamp—and it can be created in a snap.

You Will Need

- Floral foam ring with a 6"-diameter center opening
- Flowers, any desired color and sizes*
- 6"×24" cylindrical glass vase

- Food coloring, any color
- 3 large metallic plastic ornaments
- Bucket of water, wire snips

*Hydrangea and gerbera daisies were featured in Matt's version

1 Soak the floral foam ring in water for 20 minutes.

2 Cut the stems from the flowers, leaving about 2 inches of stem intact (so that you can easily insert them into the foam). Insert the flowers into the foam, positioning them so that no foam can be seen.

3 Fill the vase with water. Add food coloring until you achieve the desired color.

4 Fill the ornaments with varying amounts of water; this will cause them to rise, fall, and settle in different positions once placed in the water-filled vase. Carefully drop the ornaments into the vase, using caution so that the colored water doesn't splash (especially onto clothing and table linens).

5 Place the vase in the center of the flower-covered ring.

Pool Ball Topiaries

$46 each topiary

Designed by Erika Shay

These innovative topiaries, shown on page 220, resemble pool cues and balls. If you can't find flowers in colors that correspond to each ball, paint any variety with floral paint.

You Will Need

- 15 floral foam balls, 6" diameter

- Chicken wire

- Ribbon, brown, white, blue, any width

- Small rectangular wooden boxes

- Flowers in colors that resemble pool balls

- 15 pieces PVC pipe, 5' long and 1½" diameter

- Felt, green

- Bucket of water, hot-glue gun and glue sticks, plaster of Paris, scissors, spray adhesive, 7"-long wired floral picks, floral tape, wire snips

1 Wrap the foam balls with chicken wire; submerge in water overnight.

2 Using hot glue, attach brown ribbon to the bottom portion of the PVC pipe, white ribbon to the top portion, and blue ribbon at the tip (about 6 inches from the top of the PVC pipe) so that the PVC pipe resembles a cue stick. Following the manufacturer's instructions, mix the plaster of Paris with water; pour into the wooden boxes. Insert one piece of PVC pipe into each box; hold in place until the plaster dries. Adhere felt to the top of each box to disguise the plaster. Wrap the floral picks with the attached wire. Cover the wire with floral tape; insert the bundle into the top of the PVC pipe.

3 Cut the flower stems, leaving approximately 2 inches intact; insert the flowers into the soaked floral balls to resemble solid and striped pool balls. Attach one flower-covered ball to each PVC pipe "cue."

Wishing Tree

$115

Designed by Sally Steele

While your guests can certainly sign a guest book at your ceremony or reception, this wishing tree, shown on page 220, gives them a unique opportunity to express their feelings about you and your special day. Leave the painted circles and pens in a basket by the tree for guests to inscribe and then tie to the tree.

You Will Need

- Flowering tree, real or artificial

- 25 yards heavy twine

- Old sheets for padding the trunk

- 2 yards damask fabric, plum or other desired color

- 10 silver eyelets*

- 1 yard satin damask fabric, white or other desired color

- 3 yards satin cord, taupe or other desired color

- 50 unlined index cards, white

- Watercolor paints, any desired colors

- 2" and 2½" circle templates

- Organza ribbon with satin edging, orange or other desired colors

- Scissors, fusible hem tape, iron, ironing board, hammer, paintbrush, pencil, silver marking pen, hole punch

*Purchase eyelets with fasteners that you can place on top and under the eyelet.

1 Bind the trunk of the tree with twine to smooth out the shape of the trunk. Bind the trunk with old sheets to fill out the shape of the trunk.

2 Cut the damask fabric to a size that's large enough to wrap around trunk. Hem the edges of the fabric with fusible hem tape, following the manufacturer's instructions.

3 Install the silver eyelets on the short edges of the hemmed fabric (the edges that meet at the front of the tree trunk), spacing them approximately 4 to 5 inches apart and following the manufacturer's instructions. Generally you will cut a small hole in the fabric, slip the eyelet over and under this hole, and then place the fasteners and secure with a hammer.

4 Place the satin damask fabric on the front of the trunk lengthwise. Wrap the plum damask around the trunk so that the eyelets are lined up on the front side of the trunk. Insert the satin cord into the eyelets, lacing down the "corset" as you would tie a shoe.

5 Paint the index cards with the watercolor paint as desired; let dry. Paint the back of each card; let dry. Use the 2½-inch circle template to draw circles on the painted cards; cut out. Use the silver marking pen and the 2-inch circle template to add a silver edging to the circles. Punch a hole at the edge of each disk. Make as many painted circles as necessary for your number of guests.

6 Cut 1-foot lengths of organza ribbon (as many as you have painted circles). Thread through the hole in each circle; tie a knot to secure.

Great Idea
After the big day, remove all the well-wishes from the tree. Stash the keepsakes in a scrapbook or wedding-day time capsule.

Window Frame Altar

$235

Designed by Jackson Lowell

Whether planning an outdoor wedding and you want to frame the backdrop or you want to bring a bit of the outdoors in, this project, featured on page 219, speaks of nature and summery days.

You Will Need

- 4'× 92" wood ladder trellis

- 2 precut wooden door frame pieces, each 7½ feet long*

- 1 precut wooden door frame piece, 4 feet long*

- 4 wooden end piece accents for all four corners*

- White latex paint

- 5-foot-long wooden window box

- 20-lb. bag concrete (or other bag of heavy material; see Step 6)

- Floral foam, in size to fit into base of window box

- Flowers and filler (such as fern fronds), any color, real or artificial

- Hammer, 1-inch-long nails, wood glue, paintbrush, medium-grit sandpaper (optional), handsaw or circular saw (optional), bucket of water (optional), wire snips

*Wooden beveled door frames can be found precut or in 12-foot-long pieces that can be cut down to size at the store for a minimal cost. If you want a more finished appearance—and plan to allow the backside of the frame to show— double the amount of precut frames to finish the back in Steps 1 to 3.

1 Place the wood trellis on a flat surface. Place one precut 7½-foot-long frame piece on the right side; line it up from the top edge (the bottom of the trellis will be covered by the window box). Nail the frame piece to the trellis. Repeat on the left side of the trellis.

2 Using nails, affix the 4-foot-long frame piece to the top of the trellis.

3 Apply a liberal amount of wood glue to the back of one end piece accent; place it on one corner of the window frame. Repeat with the remaining three accent pieces. Let the glue dry completely.

4 Paint the entire constructed trellis/window frame; let dry. Paint the back of the trellis; let dry. Paint the window box, inside and out; let dry. **Optional: For a slightly distressed look, lightly sand the trellis and window box.**

5 Place the trellis in the center of the window box. **Note: You may have to trim the bottom of the trellis to fit the window box snugly.**

6 Place an unopened bag of concrete at the bottom of the window box to stabilize and weigh down the frame.

7 If using real flowers and filler, soak the foam in water for 20 minutes. Place the floral foam in the bottom of the window box. Cut the flower stems, leaving them long enough so that the flowers may be seen from above the window box. Insert the flowers into the foam and fill as desired.

Great Idea
After the ceremony, this beautiful project can pull double duty as a backdrop for the cake, buffet, or gift table.

Stenciled Aisle Runner

$75

Designed by Matt O'Dorisio

If the same old plain white runner isn't what you had in mind, use this "reverse stencil" technique, shown on page 219, to add a splash of color and pattern to your ceremony decor. If palm fronds don't complement the theme of your wedding, make paper templates of another motif that does, such as oversize flowers or your initials.

You Will Need

- Cotton or poly-cotton velvet or faux-velvet fabric, purple or other desired color*

- Several fresh palm fronds

- 24-karat gold spray paint

- Tape measure, scissors, fusible hem tape, iron, ironing board, latex gloves

*Purchase a length and width of fabric after measuring the aisle length and width at the ceremony site.

1 Cut the fabric to the needed size; hem the edges with fusible hem tape, following the manufacturer's instructions.

2 Carefully spread out the fabric on a large outdoor surface, such as a driveway, taking care to keep debris off the runner. Place the palm fronds on top of the fabric, placing them in a pleasing arrangement (randomly, around the edge, etc.).

3 While wearing latex gloves, spray around each leaf with the 24-karat gold spray paint until you have a clear silhouette of the leaf on the runner. Immediately remove each leaf; let the paint dry.

Basic Boutonniere

$5

Designed by Alan Dunn

Even if you've never worked with flowers before, you can master this easy technique in no time at all. Choose a flower that's prominent in the bride's bouquet for this quick project, shown on page 216.

You Will Need

- 1 rose or other flower, real or artificial
- Sprig of baby's breath
- Wire snips, floral tape

1 Cut the rose stem, leaving approximately 3 inches. Snip a set of leaves from the discarded stem.

2 Place the baby's breath behind the rose; place the set of leaves behind the baby's breath.

3 Using floral tape, attach the baby's breath and the leaves to the flower, starting at the base of the flower and wrapping the tape down the stem.

Quick Tip If you're using real flowers for a boutonniere, bouquet, or arrangement, you can make the project the day prior to your ceremony and store it in the refrigerator.

Cinderella Bride's Bouquet

$75

Designed by Angie Bloom Hewett

A bounty of roses makes this bouquet fit for a princess—especially with the addition of roses that have been treated to 24-karat gold accents. The bouquet, shown on page 211, is made in a holder that has a handle shaped like a scepter. Choose a handle that is comfortable to hold and complements the overall theme of your wedding.

You Will Need

- Approximately 40 roses, real or artificial*

- 24-karat gold spray paint (specially formulated for flowers)

- Bouquet holder*

- Wire snips, latex gloves, bucket of water (optional)

*If using real roses, soak the foam portion of the bouquet holder in water for 20 minutes prior to making the bouquet.

1 Cut the rose stems, leaving approximately 3 inches intact.

2 Following the manufacturer's instructions and while wearing latex gloves, paint the tips and some of the petals of about 10 roses with the 24-karat gold spray paint; let dry.

3 Starting at the top of the holder, begin to insert the roses into the foam. Work your way down and around the foam, interspersing the gold-painted roses with the natural roses.

Traditional Hand-Tied Bouquet

$50

Designed by Alan Dunn

This simple yet elegant design, featured on page 218, is perfect for a bride or bridesmaid.

You Will Need

- 5 calla lilies, real or artificial
- Ribbon, any width and color
- Floral tape, hot-glue gun, glue sticks, scissors, wire snips

1 Holding two calla lilies together, join them with floral tape. Begin taping about 4 inches below the base of the flowers; wrap the tape about 6 inches down the length of the stems.

2 Continue to add the remaining calla lilies, one at a time, to the two flowers joined in Step 1. Stagger the heights of the flowers slightly for interest.

3 Put a dab of hot glue at the base of the flowers (at the top of the floral tape). Fold over the edge of the ribbon approximately 1 inch and secure the folded edge to the hot glue. Wrap the ribbon down the length of the stem, completely covering the floral tape but leaving about 6 inches of the stems exposed. Cut the ribbon, fold over the edge 1 inch, and adhere to the stems with hot glue.

4 Trim the calla lily stems, below the taped and ribbon-covered area, so that they are about 6 inches long.

Dramatic Hand-Tied Bouquet

$⁵75

Designed by Jackson Lowell

Do you have a flair for the dramatic? If so, create a bouquet that matches your style: This showstopping arrangement, shown on page 218, features Black Magic roses, chocolate calla lilies, feathers, and a crystal drop. This bouquet would look equally as beautiful with soft pastel-color flowers or rich reds, so the choice is yours!

You Will Need

- 20 roses, any color, real or artificial

- 10 small calla lilies, real or artificial

- Long crafts feathers, any color

- Crystal sprays

- Long crystal drop (or string crystals and beads strung onto monofilament thread)

- Ribbon, any width and color

- Floral tape, hot-glue gun, glue sticks, scissors

1 Cut the rose and calla lily stems, leaving approximately 8 inches intact. Remove the leaves from the 8-inch lengths of stems.

2 Hold three roses together; this is the center of the bouquet. Using floral tape, join the three center roses, starting at the base of the flowers and wrapping about 2 inches down the stems. Continue to add roses to the center cluster, creating a round shape with the roses. Add the calla lilies to the bouquet, interspersing them throughout the roses. When all roses and lilies have been added, join the flowers with floral tape, starting at the base of the flowers and wrapping about 4 inches down the stems.

3 Add the feathers to the bouquet, around the outer edges. Join the feathers to the bouquet with floral tape, covering the ends of the feathers.

4 Insert the crystal sprays into the bouquet, interspersing them throughout the bouquet.

5 Using floral tape, adhere the crystal drop to the base of the bouquet, so that it extends past all the flower stems.

6 Put a dab of hot glue at the base of the flowers (at the top of the floral tape). Fold over the edge of the ribbon approximately 1 inch and secure the folded edge to the hot glue. Wrap the ribbon down the length of the stem, completely covering the floral tape and leaving some of the stems exposed. Cut the ribbon, fold over the edge 1 inch, and adhere to the stems with hot glue.

Quick Tip The deep red and purple feathers used to accent this bouquet lend a "Bohemian chic" look. Not your style? Consider long, graceful pheasant feathers—available at crafts stores—for a bouquet filled with harvest colors or use fluffy white feathers for a dreamy fairy-tale bouquet.

Fresh Flower Lei

$35

Designed by Angie Bloom Hewett

Planning a casual seaside wedding? If so, ditch the traditional bouquet and adorn your neck with a Hawaiian lei, as shown on page 218. The Maile lei—where the green vine Maile is featured—was historically used by the Kahuna to bind the hands of the bride and groom to symbolize their union.

You Will Need

- 3 stems of tuberose

- 15 stems of Dendrobium orchids°

- Lei string or dental floss

- Medium 12-inch-long lei needle, scissors or wire snips, tape measure

°You will need approximately 50 loose orchids for each lei.

1 Using the scissors or wire snips, cut the tuberose stems, leaving about ½ inch. Remove the stems from the orchids.

2 Cut a 90-inch length of lei string or dental floss.

3 Double-wrap the stem of one tuberose with the string; double-knot the string. This will ensure that your flowers will not slip off the string while you make the lei. Thread the needle onto the other end of the string; fold the string over about 4 inches. (This will give your thread some slack in case the needle starts to cut through.)

4 Pierce the needle through an orchid, making sure the needle goes through the nose and out the butt-end of the orchid. Alternate with the tuberose in the same fashion. **Note: Be sure to slide the flowers onto the needle first. Once the needle is full, slide the flowers down the string.**

5 Repeat Step 4 until your lei is full, leaving about 2 inches of string to tie your lei. Tie the lei into a double knot.

Lei Flower Options

The beautiful lei Angie Bloom Hewett designed—made of tuberoses and orchids—can be created with a wide variety of flowers. Consider these options:

- **Jasmine**

- **Carnations**

- **Ginger**

- **Daisies**

- **Various leaves and vines**

Bouquet Ball

$50

Designed by Matt O'Dorisio

Tired of the traditional bouquet? Create this simply stunning bouquet, shown on page 213, in minutes. This bouquet features button mums, but any small, compact flower can easily be substituted.

You Will Need

- **Approx. 50 button mums, any color**
- **4"-diameter foam ball**
- **Wire-edge ribbon, any width and color**
- **4 daisies, any color**
- **Pearl-head pins**
- **Wire snips, hot-glue gun, glue sticks, scissors, florist's wire**

1 Remove the stems from the button mums. Using the hot-glue gun and glue sticks, adhere the mums to the foam ball, leaving a small area at the top where you will attach the ribbon handle and daisies. Allow to dry.

2 Cut a piece of ribbon, approximately 1 foot long. Form a circle with the ribbon, overlapping the ends. Where the ends overlap, join the circle with a 6-inch long piece of florist's wire. Twist the wire to secure the ribbon, leaving a "tail" to insert into the foam ball. Insert the wire into the top of the foam ball; if needed, put a dab of hot glue to further secure. Allow to dry.

3 Remove the stems from the daisies. Adhere the daisies to the top of the foam ball, covering the area where the ribbon is joined to the ball. Allow to dry.

4 Insert pearl-head pins into the foam ball, in any desired locations.

Botanical Invitation

$40 for 90 invitations

Designed by Alan Dunn

With a few ordinary household materials—crayons, waxed paper, and an iron—you can create these one-of-a-kind invitations, shown on page 223.

You Will Need

- **Waxed paper**
- **Palm fronds**
- **Flower petals, any color**
- **Crayons, any color**

- **Vellum paper**
- **Scissors, wire snips, iron, heat-resistant ironing surface, straightedge, computer and printer or markers, double-stick tape**

1 Cut a piece of waxed paper approximately 2 feet long. Place on the heat-resistant ironing surface. Using scissors or wire snips, cut the palm fronds and flower petals (if removing from stems). Allow the fronds and petals to randomly drop onto the waxed paper.

2 Using scissors, "shave" the crayons, allowing the shavings to drop onto the waxed paper, over and around the fronds and petals.

3 Cut a piece of 2-foot-long waxed paper; place it on top of the botanical- and shaving-covered piece. Using an iron on low heat, iron the waxed paper "sandwich" to seal. When cool, cut the waxed paper into 4×6-inch pieces.

4 Cut the vellum paper into 3×5-inch pieces. Type and print or handwrite the message onto the vellum. Using double-stick tape, adhere one piece of vellum onto each waxed paper square.

5 Repeat Steps 1–4 until you have the desired number of invitations.

Stenciled "Lace" Invitation

$24 for 50 invitations

Designed by Jackson Lowell

Using a quick and easy stenciling technique, you can create beautiful invitations, featured on page 223, sure to impress your guests.

You Will Need

- Kraft paper
- 1 yard lace
- Spray paint, golden or other desired color
- Paper, printed with wedding-day motifs (such as roses)

- Ribbon, any width and color
- 50 paper roses
- Marker, scissors, straightedge, hole punch, computer and printer (optional), rubber cement

1 In a well-ventilated area, unroll 1 yard of kraft paper. Place the lace over the kraft paper. Using spray paint, and following the manufacturer's directions, spray the lace; remove the lace. Allow the kraft paper to dry.

2 Trace the Invitation Template **opposite** onto the kraft paper; cut out the kraft paper invitations. Using the hole punch, punch a hole in the marked "X" locations (one on each side "wing" of the invitation).

3 Cut the printed paper into 6-inch squares. Type and print or handwrite the message onto the paper. Using rubber cement, and working in a well-ventilated area, adhere the paper to the center of the invitations.

4 Fold the top and bottom side "wings" of the invitation to the center, using the straightedge to obtain crisp lines, if needed. Fold the side "wings" of the invitation to the center.

5 Cut a 15-inch length of ribbon for each invitation. Place one invitation on one piece of ribbon; bring the ribbon to the front of the invitation and thread through the punched holes. Tie a knot. Insert a paper rose into the knot.

6 Repeat Steps 1–5 until you have the desired number of invitations.

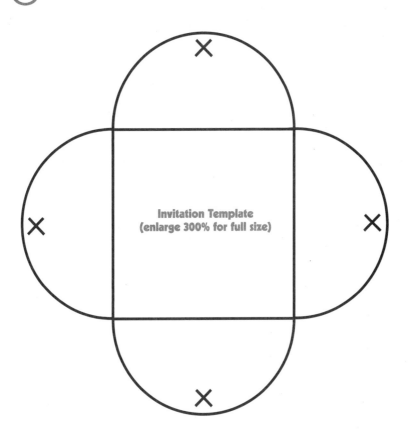

**Invitation Template
(enlarge 300% for full size)**

Index

a

accommodations, 195
aisle runner, stenciled, 240
alcoholic drinks, 106-7, 108
altar, window frame, 238-39
altar decorations, 149
alterations, 29
announcements
engagement, 54-55
wedding, 197-98
appetizers, 108
arches, flower-covered, 219
ascots, 143
attendants. See also best man;
bridesmaids; groomsmen
asking, 47
children as, 47, 54
choosing, 43, 45-47
expenses of, 47, 139
gifts for, 120
"honor," 43, 50, 164, 165, 181,
182, 185, 190
maid/matron of honor, 50, 164, 181
measurements for, 207-8
number of, 46
seating, at head table, 181
thanking, 58
ushers, 51, 145, 208
attire. See also bridal gown
for bridesmaids, 43, 134, 138-40
for flower girls, 145
for groom, 140-44
for groomsmen, 43, 140-44
measurements for, 138, 144, 207-8
for parents, 145
for ring bearer, 145
for ushers, 145

b

bachelor parties, 57
bachelorette parties, 57
bakeries, questions for, 104
balloons, 118
bands, live, 109, 110, 175
bar, cash, 107
bar, open, 107
barbecues, 98
beauty regimes, 158-59, 162-63
bed-and-breakfasts, 71
best man
duties of, 50, 164, 165, 185, 190
seating, at head table, 181
toast given by, 182
blood tests, 29, 121
botanical invitations, 249
bouquets
ball bouquet, 248
bride's, Cinderella, 242
creative ideas for, 218
hand-tied, dramatic, 244-45
hand-tied, traditional, 243
tossing, 183
types of, 116

boutonniere, basic, 241
boyfriends, former, 54
bridal gown
advice about, 34
alterations for, 29
borrowing, 135
from bridal salon, 131-33
bridesmaid dress worn as, 134
choosing, 126-31
from department store, 136
discounts on, 130, 132
dress styles, 128
extra costs for, 29
hand-sewn, 135
neckline styles, 129
from online stores, 133-34
plain, customizing, 135
previously worn, 134
renting, 134
seasonal considerations, 131
sleeve styles, 129
storing, after wedding, 199
untraditional, options for, 126
from vintage clothing store, 135
bridal salons, 131-33
bride
accessories for, 136-38
bachelorette party for, 57
beauty regimes, 158-59
bridal showers for, 57, 59
children of, 54, 154-55, 196
divorced, 155
escorting down aisle, 51-52
expenses of, 162
maiden name, changing, 122, 198
measurements for, 207
personal attendant for, 52
in receiving line, 158
seating, at head table, 181
toast given by, 182
widowed, 155
bride's parents
attire for, 145
duties of, 51-52
expenses of, 23, 42, 51-52
gifts for, 120
bridesmaids
accessories for, 140
asking, 47
beauty regime, 162
choosing, 43, 45-47
dresses, 134, 138-40
duties of, 51
expenses of, 47, 139
gifts for, 120
measurements for, 207
number of, 46
thanking, 58
brunch, 97, 98, 169, 172
budget
preparing, 25
updating, 58
worksheet for, 202-3
buffets, 97, 98, 107

c

cakes
advice about, 34
alternatives to, 106
choosing, tips for, 105-6
cost estimates, 105
cutting, 182
decorating, ideas for, 221
flavor and taste, 108, 176
frostings for, 102
glossary of terms, 102
groom's cake, 105
hidden costs of, 77
homemade, 106
nontraditional, 106
serving sizes, 105-6
sheet cakes, 105
from small bakeries, 105
styles, 103
undecorated, toppers for, 108
calligraphy, 89
cameras, disposable, 178
candles, 118, 173
candles, champagne flute, 226-27
cash, paying expenses with, 25
cash bar, 107
castles, renting, 63-64
caterers, 99-101
choosing, 100
friends and relatives, 101
grocery stores, 101
nonprofit groups, 101
questions to ask, 100
restaurants, 99, 101
tearooms, 101
centerpieces, 112, 224, 234
ceremony. See also ceremony site;
officiant
items to bring to, 164-65
itinerary for, 160-61, 164
Jewish, 68, 157, 219, 228-29
marriage license for, 29, 121-22,
152-53
music for, 149, 155
premarital classes, 150
processional, 156, 157
programs for, 87, 92-93, 222-23
recessional, 157
seating at, 157
send-off from, 156
special tributes at, 155-56
vows, 153-55
ceremony site
booking date for, 84
city hall or courthouse, 82
creative ideas for, 79-82
decorations at, 35, 149-50, 174,
219, 220
flowers at, 113, 174
holding reception at, 80-82, 84
licenses and permits for, 29
"no cost," about, 84
nontraditional, precautions for, 65, 73
parking permits for, 29

questions to ask about, 81, 83
selecting, 21, 81, 83
traditional, 82
transportation to, 71, 120-21
visiting, 82-84
chairs, 77, 174
champagne flute candles, 226-27
charity, donations to, 57, 177
checking account, joint, 28
checklist, floral needs, 113
checklist, timeline, 38-40
cheese trays, 108
children
assigning roles to, 42
of bride, 54, 154-55, 196
flower girls, 47, 51, 145, 207
of groom, 54, 196
including in vows, 154-55
as junior attendants, 47, 54
meals for, 108
ring bearers, 47, 51, 145, 164, 208
chuppah, decorative, 228-29
church weddings, 81, 82, 149
Cinderella bride's bouquet, 242
city hall, 82
civil ceremony, 82
classes, premarital, 150
coats and jackets, 142
cocktail-style reception, 98, 169
collars, shirt, 143
college campuses, 63
commodity organizations, 101
confetti, 173
consultants. **See** wedding planners
contracts, 78
corkage fees, 77, 107
couples showers, 59
credit cards, 28, 76-77
cummerbunds, 143

d

dance, first, 52
dancing, 179, 182
date, wedding, 19, 84
death certificate, 121
decorations
at ceremony, 35, 149-50, 174,
219, 220
champagne flute candles, 226-27
decorative chuppah, 228-29
lava lamp centerpiece, 234
palm tree decoration, 232-33
photographs used as, 173
stenciled aisle runner, 240
window frame altar, 238-39
wishing tree, 236-37
zen fountain, 230-31
delegating tasks, 45, 49, 58, 148, 183
department-store dresses, 136
deposit money, 28
destination weddings
legal details, 70, 82, 153
places to consider, 70-71
pros and cons of, 70
save the date cards for, 86
transportation to, 71
dinner, rehearsal, 119
dinners, sit-down, 97, 98, 108

disk jockeys, 110, 175
divorce decree, 121
divorced bride, 155
divorced groom, 155
divorced parents, 43, 53, 157, 158
donations, charitable, 57, 177
dresses. See also bridal gown
bridesmaid, 134, 138-40
flower girl, 145
for mothers, 145
drinks, 106-7, 108

e

emcees, 175
engagement announcement, 54-55
engagement parties, 57, 59
engraving, 87, 89
entertainment, 179, 182. **See also**
music
entrées, choosing, 108
ethnic traditions, 66-69
expenses
for bride, 162
for bridesmaids, 139
for bride's parents, 23, 42, 51-52
for groom's parents, 23, 42, 52, 119
hidden, sources of, 28-29, 77-78
for one-of-a-kind weddings, 65, 73
paying up, 198
payment methods, 25, 28, 76-77,
190
tracking, methods for, 45
worksheet for, 24

f

facials, 163
family. See also parents
as attendants, 46
blended, on honeymoon, 196
blended, vows for, 154-55
elderly relatives, 73
former spouses, 54
and guest list, 41, 44
in receiving line, 158
seating, at ceremony, 157
seating, at reception, 181
stepbrothers, 54
stepparents, 54
stepsisters, 54
fathers
attire for, 145
measurements for, 208
in receiving line, 158
stepfathers, 52, 53
favors, party, 177, 179-80
fees. **See** expenses
finances. **See** expenses; money
florists, 114, 115
flower girls
attire for, 145
choosing, 47
duties of, 51
measurements for, 207
flowers, 111-18. **See also** bouquets
advice about, 34-35
alternatives to, 118
basic boutonniere, 241

centerpieces, 112, 224
for ceremony site, 113, 174
checklist for, 113
choosing, 112-15, 149
color of, 118
dried or artificial, 112
fragrant, 115
fresh flower lei, 246-47
giving away, 191
pick-your-own, 111, 174
prioritizing, 112
renting, 118, 149
in season, 112, 149, 173
food. See also cakes; menus
advice about, 35
brunch, 97, 98, 169, 172
buffets, 97, 98, 107
caterers, 99-101
importance of, 97, 177, 178
leftover, 191
matching with wedding style, 98
prior to ceremony, 165
servers for, 53
sit-down dinners, 97, 98, 108
formalwear shops, 141
fountain, zen, 230-31
frostings, types of, 102

g

garter toss, 182-83
gifts
charitable donations, 57, 177
monetary, 25
registering for, 56-57
thank-you notes for, 87, 88, 196-
97
for wedding party, 120
girlfriends, former, 54
global traditions, 66-69
gloves, 138, 140
gratuities, 28, 29, 164-65
grocery stores, catering by, 101
groom
accessories for, 143
attire for, 140-44
bachelor party for, 57
beauty regimes, 158-59, 162-63
children of, 54, 196
divorced, 155
groom's cake, 105
measurements for, 208
in receiving line, 158
seating, at head table, 181
toast given by, 182
widowed, 155
groom's parents
attire for, 145
duties of, 52, 119
expenses of, 23, 42, 52, 119
gifts for, 120
groomsmen
accessories for, 143
asking, 47
attire for, 43, 140-44
choosing, 43, 45-47
duties of, 51
expenses of, 47, 139
gifts for, 120

measurements for, 208
number of, 46
thanking, 58
guests
accommodations for, 195
compiling list of, 37, 41, 42, 44
fallback list of, 41
guest book for, 52
honorary, 53
number of, 19
parents' guests, 44
for reception only, 86
relatives, 41, 42
seating, at ceremony, 157
seating, at reception, 181
thanking, 58
for wedding only, 86

h

hair, washing and styling, 159, 162
headpieces, 136-37, 140
home weddings, 80, 172
honeymoon, 194-96
honor attendants
duties of, 50, 164, 165, 185, 190
meaning of term, 43
seating, at head table, 181
toast given by, 182
honorariums, 164-65
honorary guests, 53

i

insurance, wedding, 122-23
invitations
botanical, 249
creative ideas for, 222-23
handwritten, 88
proofreading, 90
for reception only, 86
for rehearsal dinner, 119
stenciled "lace," 250-51
for wedding only, 86
when to mail, 88
wording for, 90-91
worksheet for, 206
itinerary, for ceremony, 160-61, 164
itinerary, for reception, 188-89

j

jackets and coats, 142
jewelry, 136
Jewish ceremonies, 68, 157, 219,
228-29

l

laser printing, 89
lava lamp centerpiece, 234
legal details
blood tests, 29, 121
death certificate, 121
for destination weddings, 70, 82, 153
divorce decree, 121
legal will, 122
liquor license, 29, 107
marriage certificate, 70, 121-22,
152-53, 164, 198

marriage license, 29, 121-22, 152-53
name change, 122, 198
parking permits, 29
wedding insurance, 122-23
lei, fresh flower, 246-47
license, marriage, 29, 121-22, 152-53
lights, reception, 173
liquor license, 29, 107
location. **See** ceremony site; reception site

m

maid/matron of honor, 50, 164, 181
maiden names, 122, 198
makeup, 162
manicures, 163
marriage certificate, 70, 121-22,
152-53, 164, 198
marriage license, 29, 121-22,
152-53
massages, 163
measurements
accurate, importance of, 138, 144
worksheet for, 207-8
menus
brunch, 97, 98, 169, 172
buffets, 97, 98, 107
choosing, tips for, 107-8
planning worksheet for, 205
simple, 177
sit-down dinners, 97, 98, 108
take-out, restaurant, 101
money. See also expenses
bride's and groom's, 23
budgets, 25, 58
budget worksheet, 202-3
for deposits, 28
from gifts, 25
from parents, 23
sources of, 23-25
spending habits quiz, 26-27
mothers
attire for, 145
beauty regime, 162
measurements for, 207
in receiving line, 158
music
at ceremony, 149, 155
disk jockeys, 110, 175
live bands, 109, 110, 175
overtime charges, 77, 111
at reception, 35, 174-76
restrictions on, 149

n

nails, 163
name, changing, 122, 198
newspaper announcements, 55, 197-98
nonprofit organizations, 101

o

officiant
choosing, 150-52
discussing rehearsal with, 119
duties of, 121-22, 152-53
honorarium for, 164-65
questions to ask, 151
vows suggested by, 154

offset printing, 89
online bridal gowns, 133-34
online registry, 56
online resources, 78-79
open bar, 107
organizational system, 45
outdoor weddings, 70-71, 80
overtime charges, 77, 111

p

package deals, 77
palm tree decoration, 232-33
parents
attire for, 145
bride's, duties of, 51-52, 158
bride's, expenses of, 23, 42, 51-52
divorced, 43, 53, 157, 158
fathers, 145, 158, 208
gifts for, 120
groom's, duties of, 52, 119, 158
groom's, expenses of, 23, 42, 52,
119
influence on guest list, 44
mothers, 145, 158, 162, 207
in receiving line, 158
stepfathers, 52, 53
stepparents, 54, 145, 155, 158
thanking, 58
toasts given by, 182
parking permits, 29
parties
bachelor, 57
bachelorette, 57
bridal showers, 57, 59
couples showers, 59
engagement, 57, 59
party favors, 177, 179-80
pasta dishes, 108
pedicures, 163
personal attendant, for bride, 52
photographers, 93-96
advice about, 34
amateur, 93, 95, 178
choosing, 94, 95-96
fees charged by, 95
questions to ask, 94
scheduling time for, 96
venue restrictions and, 96
photographs, 93-96
black and white, 95, 198
candid, 178
decorating with, 173
for engagement announcement, 55
of guests, 179
number of, 95
style of, 95
traditional, 179
for wedding announcement, 198
picnics, 98
plants, potted, 113, 149
potlucks, 98, 172
premarital classes, 150
printing, offset and laser, 89
priorities
establishing, 18-21, 22
focusing on, 58
worksheet for, 20
processional details, 157
programs, wedding, 87, 92-93, 222-23

projects
basic boutonniere, 241
botanical invitation, 249
bouquet ball, 248
champagne flute candles, 226-27
Cinderella bride's bouquet, 242
decorative chuppah, 228-29
dramatic hand-tied bouquet, 244-45
fresh flower lei, 246-47
lava lamp centerpiece, 234
palm tree decoration, 232-33
pool ball topiaries, 235
stenciled aisle runner, 240
stenciled "lace" invitation, 250-51
traditional hand-tied bouquet, 243
window frame altar, 238-39
wishing tree, 236-37
zen fountain, 230-31

r

receiving line, 158, 180-81
reception. See also food; menus;
    reception site
bouquet toss at, 183
cutting cake at, 182
dancing at, 182
date of, 169
departing from, 185, 190
drinks at, 106-7
end of, 190-91
entertainment at, 179, 182
garter toss at, 182-83
head table at, 181
hosts, duties of, 52
itinerary for, 188-89
music, 35, 174-76
party favors at, 179-80
receiving line at, 158, 180-81
seating at, 181
style of, 170-71
timeline for, 186-87
time of day, 169, 172
toasts given at, 182
reception site
ambiance of, 21
booking date for, 84
choosing, 21, 81, 85
cleaning up, 191
creative ideas for, 79-80, 82
decorations at, 35, 172-74
flowers for, 174
holding ceremony at, 80-82, 84
licenses and permits for, 29
"no cost," about, 84
nontraditional, 65, 73, 169
questions to ask about, 81, 85
traditional, 169
transportation to, 35, 71, 120-21
visiting, 82-84
recessional details, 157
rehearsal and rehearsal dinner, 119
restaurants, 99, 101
ring bearers
attire for, 145
choosing, 47
duties of, 51, 164
measurements for, 208
rings, 51, 164
rooftop settings, 65

s

salons, bridal, 131-33
sample sales, 132
save the date cards, 86, 88
seating, at ceremony, 157
seating, at reception, 181
servers, 53
shirt collars, 143
shoes, 138, 140, 144
shopping strategies, 76-79
showers, for bride or couple, 57, 59
skin care, 163
socks, 144
spending habits, quiz for, 26-27
spouses, former, 54
stationery
calligraphy, 89
choosing, 87
do-it-yourself, 92-93
engraving for, 87, 89
laser printing, 89
offset printing, 89
personalizing, 92-93
thermography, 89
stenciled aisle runner, 240
stenciled "lace" invitations, 250-51
stepbrothers, 54
stepfathers, 52, 53
stepparents, 54, 145, 155, 158
stepsisters, 54
surprise weddings, 72
survival kit, 165
synagogues, 82

t

tables
centerpieces for, 112, 224, 234
decorating, 172, 174
head table, 181
tearooms, 101
thank-you notes, 87, 88, 196-97
theme weddings
affair to remember theme, 216
autumn theme, 64
black and white theme, 65-66
candy land theme, 217
fairy tale theme, 63-64, 210-11
groovy '60s theme, 212-13
holiday theme, 64
"I Dream of Jeannie" theme, 215
1950s Havana theme, 65, 214
precautions about, 73
rooftop settings, 65
school theme, 63
at site of marriage proposal, 72
sports theme, 64
surprise weddings, 72
winter theme, 64
thermography, 89
ties, 143, 144
time-management tips, 44-45
timelines
checklist for, 38-40
establishing, 44
for reception, 186-87
tips and gratuities, 28, 29, 164-65
toasts, at reception, 182, 184
traditions, ethnic, 66-69

transportation, 35, 71, 120-21
tuxedos, 142-43, 144, 145

u

ushers, 51, 145, 208

v

vegetarian meals, 98, 108
veils, 136-37
vendor contact information, 204
vests, 143
videographers, 34, 96-97
videography, 96-97, 179
vintage designer dresses, 135
vows, 153-55

w

wedding announcements, 197-98
wedding planners
benefits of, 31-37
choosing, 33, 37
for day of wedding, 148
for destination weddings, 153
fees charged by, 30
questions to ask, 33
wedding programs, 87, 92-93
    222-23
wills, 122
window frame altar, 238-39
wine, buying, 108
wine corkage fees, 77, 107
wineries, 71
wishing tree, 236-37
worksheets and tests
allocating expenses, 24
balancing family and friends,
    42-43
budget breakdown, 202-3
ceremony itinerary, 160-61
dos and don'ts, 58
floral needs checklist, 113
formalwear measurements,
    207-8
invitations, 206
menu planning, 205
reception itinerary, 188-89
reception styles, 170-71
reception timeline, 186-87
setting priorities, 20
spending habits test, 26-27
timeline checklist, 38-40
vendor contact information, 204

z

zen fountain, 230-31

Resources

Alan Dunn
Tres L.A. Catering
5959 Franklin Ave. Ste. 109
Hollywood, CA 90028
Phone: 323/466-1835
Fax: 323/466-1875
Website: www.tresla.com

Angie Bloom Hewett
Moments in Bloom
Phone: 805/577-8476
Website: www.momentsinbloom.com

Jackson Lowell
Jackson Studios
c/o NSM Management
P.O. Box 5055
Beverly Hills, CA 90209
Phone: 310/390-8125

Matt O'Dorisio
Matt O'Dorisio Design
Website: www.mattodorisio.com

Erika Shay
The Princess Bride
Phone: 845/708-3234
Website: www.theprincessbride.com

Sally Steele
Website: www.sallysteele.net